Understanding Panic and Other Anxiety Disorders

Understanding Health and Sickness Series
Miriam Bloom, Ph.D.
General Editor

Understanding Panic and Other Anxiety Disorders

Benjamin A. Root

University Press of Mississippi
Jackson

www.upress.state.ms.us

Illustrations by Regan Causey Tuder.

Library of Congress Cataloging-in-Publication Data

Root, Benjamin A.
   Understanding panic and other anxiety disorders / Benjamin A.
Root
      p.   cm.—(Understanding health and sickness series)
      Includes index.
      ISBN 1-57806-244-6 (cloth : alk. paper)—ISBN 1-57806-245-4
   (pbk. : alk. paper)
      1. Panic disorders.   2. Anxiety.   I. Title.   II. Series.
   RC535.R66   2000
   616.85′233—dc21   00-021977

British Library Cataloging-in-Publication Data available

A man who fears suffering is already suffering from what he fears.

—Michel de Montaigne

Contents

Introduction

Just over two decades ago, the idea of an emotional disturbance called panic disorder was officially introduced into common discussion among psychiatrists. Since that time much research, revision, and dissemination of knowledge have been undertaken regarding a group of disorders that are now fairly well recognized. Diverse studies indicate that 1.5 to 3.5 percent of the population experience panic disorder at some point in their lives, and many other people are afflicted with related disorders, such as social phobia, generalized anxiety disorder, depression, bipolar disorder, posttraumatic stress disorder, and specific phobia.

It's estimated that in the United States somewhere between three and six million people are affected by panic disorder. Although cultural differences allow for a variety of symptom patterns, the incidence of the disorder doesn't vary much according to social class or race. Women get panic disorder about twice as often as men. The disorder tends to make its initial appearance when a person is a young adult, but it can occur for the first time at any age. It is believed that about 70 to 90 percent of patients suffering from panic disorder will show significant improvement with appropriate treatment.

Symptoms of panic disorder were generally underreported and underrecognized by persons in the medical profession until fairly recently. Many people who were suffering sought help in emergency rooms and doctors' offices, undergoing all manner of general examinations and laboratory tests to rule out various medical conditions. Frequently, nothing could be discovered to explain the difficulties, with the result that people were dismissed without adequate treatment. (Part of the problem in diagnosing panic disorder is that its symptoms mimic those of other, nonpsychiatric, conditions.) In fact, not much in the way of pharmacological treatment was available for this disorder until the last two decades, but in recent years a number of medications have appeared on the market to the benefit of those suffering from this often disabling affliction.

This book is designed for people who are interested in learning about panic disorder and related syndromes. I begin by describing the symptoms of panic disorder, discussing related conditions, and explaining panic attacks and the gradual refinement of our understanding of them. Next comes a review of the prevalence of the disorder and what researchers believe causes it, followed by a look at treatments. The book ends with a chapter on recent research.

Since no book can take the place of the individual attention provided by a doctor, I urge anyone who may be suffering from a psychiatric problem to seek help from a psychiatrist without delay.

Understanding Panic and Other Anxiety Disorders

1. The Nature of Panic Disorder

Emergency room doctors have always puzzled over the symptoms presented by patients, but the cases of those suffering from the anxiety disorders have been especially perplexing. Persons affected by panic attacks, in addition to experiencing profound fear and feelings of discomfort, usually have symptoms that could be cardiac, respiratory, neurological, or endocrinological. Appearing without any clear-cut precipitating factors, these episodes occur unexpectedly and repeatedly, so that patients usually end up seeing numerous specialists in an attempt to rule out a variety of general medical disorders.

The terms used to describe psychiatric disorders have changed over the years. During the American Civil War, Dr. Jacob Mendes DaCosta described finding in soldiers what he believed to be a cardiovascular disorder involving chest pains and palpitations of the heart, but, as it turned out, actual heart disease was not usually present. This syndrome became known as neurocirculatory asthenia and was also called effort syndrome, cardiac neurosis, soldier's heart, and DaCosta's syndrome. It was often associated with the emotional and physical trauma of war.

Sigmund Freud used the term "anxiety neurosis" to describe a variety of anxiety-related symptoms, some taking the form of chronic, persistent anxiety and others character-ized by "sudden onslaughts of anxiety," a pattern to which we would probably apply the term "panic attack." Freud's theories went through several stages of development, and a later one involved the idea that anxiety came from the threat posed by unacceptable libidinal wishes finding their way into the conscious mind. Partly as a result of the biological turn that psychiatry has taken, many mental health professionals have come to regard Freud's theories as obsolete, but he was a keen observer who, after all, felt that "biology is destiny."

During and between the twentieth century's two world wars, people with symptoms of panic disorder gradually came to be treated less frequently by those in the field of internal medicine and more often by psychiatrists. Observers of psychiatric disorders had early on distinguished between what we now know as panic disorder and agoraphobia, but, in spite of such historical observations, for many years agoraphobia was regarded as just another phobia without any special relation to panic disorder.

The central characteristic of panic disorder is that of having distinct episodes of intense anxiety, which develop abruptly and seemingly lack an adequate precipitating factor. These episodes tend to reach maximum intensity over a period of a few minutes and last for an unpredictable period of time. The notion of an "adequate" precipitating event is important, since the sufferers inevitably get the impression that certain situations contribute to the onset of an attack, so that they frequently start limiting activities in order to keep out of emotional harm's way. Those who have had panic attacks report that they have never had any experience quite so terrifying. Frequently, however, they seem at a loss as to how to express the exact emotional ingredients. It is apparently difficult for someone who has never had such an attack to understand the impact. (It is sometimes helpful for doctors to talk to patients who only have episodes of increased anxiety in order to be able to differentiate these from genuine panic attacks.)

Another of the hallmarks of panic disorder is a persistent worry that a panic attack may occur, and this unpredictability typically causes additional consternation to those affected. Some people may worry excessively about their health, since they feel that something is "really wrong," or they may become preoccupied with modifying their behavior in an effort to guarantee that a panic attack won't happen. Those with simple generalized anxiety disorder don't show that degree of interepisodic dread of recurring attacks, and neither do people who have occasional panic attacks that fall short of the full-blown syndrome.

When a panic attack strikes for the first time, patients are characteristically at a complete loss as to what is going on. They frequently, but not always, end up in the emergency room. Many of them have a tendency to self-medicate with alcohol or other substances, which seldom helps and frequently leads to trouble. They often have to stop work and are unable to function as usual in their families. They frequently give up driving, since that is for many an anxiety-laden activity. Shopping also seems to present problems for many of these patients, probably because it involves frustration and a great deal of sensory input, as does driving.

Typical of panic attacks are symptoms usually associated with heart problems, such as palpitations, a racing pulse, and a pounding sensation in the chest, as well as, sometimes, actual chest pain. These kinds of symptoms, along with shortness of breath and a sensation of choking, are what precipitate many trips to the emergency room. Those affected also frequently complain of profuse sweating, trembling or shaking, nausea and dizziness, numbness and tingling sensations, and hot and cold flashes. Symptoms are frequently complicated by feelings of derealization (the sense that the environment is not real) and depersonalization (the sense that the individual himself or herself is not real). Additionally, persons may fear that they are losing control or "going crazy."

Panic attacks can occur as part of any of the psychiatric disorders and in a number of medical conditions, including thyroid and other endocrine disorders, as well as being associated with substance withdrawal, cardiac, pulmonary, and neurological problems. The three types of panic attacks are (1) those that are totally unexpected, (2) those that almost always happen with some specific situational provocation, and (3) those whose probability is increased with some specific situational provocation. At least some of the panic attacks must be totally unexpected before a person can be said to have panic disorder, with or without agoraphobia. This doesn't mean that the other two types are not present as well. As the illness progresses, people are often subject to panic attacks resulting from certain situations, especially after they have become aware of the potential for one to occur.

Frequently, people suffering from panic disorder describe their first attack as having come on totally "out of the blue" during some mundane activity such as shopping or working at their desks, and afterward they are unable to feel secure when they are engaged in those tasks. It is, in fact, the un-predictable nature of the acute episode which contributes so strongly to the interepisodic anxiety and avoidant coping strategies. Panic attacks may occur at night, waking people up from sleep, or the first thing in the morning. Such a situation can contribute to insomnia or even a fear of going to sleep. Many clinicians and researchers feel that panic attacks are related to the body's natural "fight or flight" mechanism, which is considered adaptive when the person is faced with some sort of external life-or-death situation, but which only contributes to additional stress when it is set off without adequate provocation.

When someone shows up in an emergency room complain-ing of symptoms such as those described above, the physician there first makes sure that nothing is going on from a cardiac, respiratory, or neurological standpoint that would require spe-cific, nonpsychiatric treatment. The tests that are administered can be expensive and time-consuming but are nonetheless necessary to rule out disorders of a general medical nature. Patients who come away from the emergency room with test results that are only superficially reassuring may have the unsettling feeling that no one has a clear picture of what has happened to them and that, in all likelihood, whatever it was will recur, because it hasn't been treated.

Panic attacks usually do recur, and, after a time, patients may begin to feel a lack of confidence in the medical system. They frequently return to the same emergency room, often when the same doctor is on duty. The staff at the emergency room may have begun to recognize the patient and to suspect that something of a psychiatric nature is going on. The patient starts to dread going to the emergency room, realizing that it will probably involve more tests leading down blind alleys and more of the disconcerting feeling that nothing's going to help. Sometimes the patient is embarrassed enough to seek help at a different emergency room, and, in so doing, complicates the situation even more, since the personnel there are unlikely to know what examinations have already been done.

Many emergency room personnel and much of the general public tend to regard symptoms of an emotional nature in a dismissive way that makes getting help difficult, and the propensity for stigmatizing psychiatric illness has contributed to the problem. Doctors are inclined to react toward conditions such as heart attacks and pneumonia in one way and toward what seem to be panic attacks in another. (This is not universally true, of course, but it helps to be aware of the general situation.)

In many cases, patients themselves try to avoid the idea that they might have a psychiatric condition, feeling uneasy with the notion that something might be wrong with them emotionally. Many doctors and other health care workers are reluctant to discuss psychiatric matters with patients for the same reason. Unfortunately, the stigma is hard to get past. Much of the discomfort has to do with a general lack of familiarity regarding psychiatric disturbances on the part of both hospital staff and the patient. It is also hard to convince patients that they have a psychiatric disorder when the symptoms seem so obviously physical. To a doctor who has seen panic disorder enough times, however, the symptom pattern is clear, and other explanations don't fit.

Part of the problem leading all concerned down blind alleys is the misconception that panic attacks do not occur unless something sufficiently anxiety-provoking has happened. However, one of the hallmarks of a panic attack is precisely that: the lack of an adequate external precipitating event. One of the ironies discussed by the psychologist William James is that, because of human beings' position in the present world, we have, in general, less cause for justified panic reactions in our lives. Some researchers speculate that panic attacks represent some sort of cognitive-emotional substitution brought on by our lack of exposure to the naturally occurring dangers that confronted our ancestors. Charles Darwin also puzzled over the causes and natural consequences of our tendency to be afraid.

Many times patients leave the emergency department confused, because, although they've been given a list of all the maladies they *don't* have, they have not received an adequate explanation of what the problem is. Many find it hard to believe that the symptoms occurring in panic disorder can be caused by the mind, even though a physician may have said as much; they are convinced that some condition must exist to explain symptoms that are so intense and physical in nature. (The saying "It's all in your head" is a great hurdle to overcome, since the usual implication is that symptoms are imaginary or not worth anyone's attention. Paradoxically, problems "in the head" are among the most painful and difficult to treat; in fact, many patients believe that any such problem is automatically untreatable.)

Panic disorder tends to go through several different phases as it develops. In one of these, patients appear hypochondriacal. They start worrying, imagining that they have various physical illnesses, usually serious ones, and that explains their puzzling symptoms. This phase often disappears as the condition becomes clearer. A patient may develop a phobia—

a persistent, unreasonable dread of some situation or object—that is severe enough to interfere with his or her life. Sometimes these phobias are specific, such as fear of flying, of certain animals, or of heights. In other cases, the patients develop a dread of any social situation in which they might somehow humiliate themselves. These tendencies toward phobia often fade away, although agoraphobic tendencies—those involving fear of leaving the home—frequently persist and become a central feature of the disorder. Sometimes people develop specific phobias because they have a sense of cause and effect regarding the situation in which they had the first panic attack; at other times, however, the phobias have no discernible link to the first occurrence. It may happen that a long-standing phobia, such as a fear of snakes, will become more severe with the onset of panic disorder, but it may also be the case that the object of dread is something that has never previously bothered the patient.

Agoraphobia

Agoraphobia is a disorder closely related to panic disorder. In fact, the two conditions occur together so often that many experts consider agoraphobia to be a complication of panic disorder. Those with agoraphobia have a fear of being in places where extricating themselves or getting assistance would be next to impossible. (The term comes from the Greek word for "market"; symptoms are frequently associated with a person's being in public places.)

People with this disorder begin to steer clear of what they see as potential anxiety triggers until they have severely restricted their activities and can no longer function; they may start by avoiding one particular situation, but then become unable to leave the house or even a certain room in the house. Transportation can become a problem, with patients being afraid to drive, although they may be all right if someone else is doing so. Sometimes the condition involves just a fear of driving alone in the car or of driving in private vehicles, while at other times the fear centers on public conveyances. Although there is a range of symptoms, a common one is fear of crowds and of public places, such as large stores or shopping malls. Often patients will avoid any situation felt to be unpredictable. They may also have a fear of embarrassment, though not to the same degree as that found in social phobia (see chapter 2).

People with agoraphobia often find themselves in a gradually constricting "comfort zone" that is strictly geographic in nature. They may find it impossible, for example, to go more than two or three blocks from their home without great discomfort. They may be unable to get to work or to perform if they are there. They frequently have to call on friends and family to help them get around, and they become dependent on those people. Such a situation can turn out to be inconvenient and stressful, not just for the patients but also for those who have volunteered to help out. Persons already impeded by panic attacks may find themselves subject to additional restrictions if they also have agoraphobia.

In actuality, almost all persons suffering from agoraphobia (about 95 percent) also have a history of panic disorder, but there are cases in which the agoraphobia exists independently. It is estimated from community samples that between one-third and one-half of patients suffering from panic disorder also have agoraphobia.

2. Some Related Disorders

Related to panic disorder and its associated syndrome of agoraphobia are several other conditions with varying patterns of anxiety and despondency, which need to be differentiated from panic disorder. Sometimes the symptoms of anxiety and panic attacks are the result of one of these conditions rather than of panic disorder.

Generalized Anxiety Disorder

Generalized anxiety disorder is a pattern of persistent worry and anxiety that continues for at least six months. People with this condition worry and feel anxious about various activities or events, and, to some degree, their symptoms interfere with their daily lives. Typical symptoms include general restlessness with insomnia and easy fatigability with difficulty in concentrating. Sometimes patients fear they may be developing Alzheimer's disease, because they do not remember incidents that have occurred around them; the reason for this, however, is that they were not able to pay adequate attention. Patients also typically report headaches and backaches that follow from the muscle tension often associated with this disorder. Affected people frequently have sleeping difficulties—trouble going to sleep, staying asleep, or just achieving restful sleep, and they may be irritable. Sometimes those suffering from generalized anxiety disorder will report "panicky" sensations, but usually they are referring to sporadic increases in the level of generalized anxiety. A reason for differentiating between generalized anxiety disorder and panic disorder is that different treatments are used (see chapter 5).

Obsessive-Compulsive Disorder

Obsessive-compulsive disorder is characterized by the presence of obsessions or compulsions or both. Obsessions are unwelcome thoughts, images, or impulses that cause a person distress; however, if a person with this disorder tries to suppress such thoughts, even greater distress results. Typically, compulsions are repetitive behaviors, often driven by obsessions or by certain rules that the patient has established to avoid some sort of dreaded, yet unrealistic, consequence. At some point during the course of this disorder, patients realize that the obsessions or compulsions are unreasonable. Although symptoms interfere with everyday life, people are frequently reluctant to seek psychiatric or medical help because they are embarrassed by the condition, and may even have the impression that they alone are suffering from it.

Posttraumatic Stress Disorder

This problem involves the consequences of an emotionally damaging event through which someone has gone, such as having one's life threatened, being present at someone's death, or having serious injury done to oneself or others, resulting in fear and the person's sense that he or she is helpless to prevent some tragedy. Symptoms disturb the patient's life, and last for a significant length of time (at least one month). The fear and sense of helplessness are reexperienced by the patient, usually in recollections of the traumatic event, including intrusive thoughts and recurring dreams. Also typical are what have come to be known as "flashbacks," in which the person has a sense of reliving the event. Patients characteristically become distressed if anything, such as a movie, a television program, reading matter, or a conversation, reminds them of the traumatic event. Their response is to try to avoid whatever might trigger a tendency to "replay the tape." Sometimes they complain about what seems to be a memory deficit regarding some part of the painful incident, and they report a sense of emotional numbing, with a generally decreased level of involvement in things that used to interest them and feelings of detachment from those around them. They frequently show a blunted range of emotions and regard the future bleakly, having difficulty picturing a life of normal length. Other symptoms characteristic of posttraumatic stress disorder are decreased sleep, diminished concentration, and a tendency to be startled easily. Affected persons may be overly vigilant, constantly expecting that something bad is going to happen to themselves or to others. They suffer from a high level of general frustration.

Acute Stress Disorder and Brief Psychotic Disorder

Acute stress disorder also involves the emotional reactions of patients to traumatic events, but differs from posttraumatic stress disorder in at least two ways. One is that acute stress disorder includes symptoms of dissociation, that is, feelings of detachment from or numbness to surroundings, difficulty in remembering events around the time of the trauma, or a sense of derealization or depersonalization (the feeling that things around the affected persons or they themselves aren't real). A second distinguishing feature is that this acute disorder lasts for no more than four weeks, whereas post-traumatic stress disorder, which must be present for at least that long to be so called, can theoretically last forever. Related to acute stress disorder and posttraumatic stress disorder is a condition known as brief psychotic disorder, which is a disturbance lasting less than one month and also characterized by delusions (false beliefs), hallucinations (false perceptions), disorganized speech and/or behavior, or even catatonia. Brief psychotic disorder is sometimes, but not always, preceded by a traumatic event.

Social Phobia

A disorder that is finally getting some much-needed attention is social phobia, also called social anxiety disorder. Persons with this condition have a pervasive fear that they will somehow humiliate themselves in a social or performance situation. Patients characteristically learn to avoid the situations that almost always cause them to experience anxiety, and their lives sometimes become quite restricted as a consequence. There is much overlap between this problem and panic disorder, since panic attacks frequently occur as a part of social phobia. (These two disorders do not include symptoms that are more consistent with some other psychiatric condition or are the result of a general medical condition or of substance abuse.) The fears of patients with social phobia can become so generalized that they see almost all social situations as threatening and may try to avoid socializing entirely. It's important to distinguish social phobia from simple shyness, which is not pathological and does not interfere with patients' lives. (Perhaps "pathological shyness" should be an alternative diagnostic label for social phobia.) Patients with social phobia tend to isolate themselves and generally have few friends. They assume that no one else suffers from similar symptoms, and their embarrassment may isolate them even more. This disorder tends to occur about twice as often in women as in men, although statistics are confusing, because, apparently, a higher percentage of men seek help. Patients with this disorder have trouble with a variety of endeavors, including school and work, and often end up doing poorly in these settings because of a general fear of embarrassment, which may then lead them to begin avoiding such places.

Research regarding social phobia indicates that the limbic system (the major emotion-related system in the brain) may play a major role, with at least some of the neurochemistry of the disorder having to do with serotonin function. (Serotonin is one of the neurotransmitters, or chemicals in the brain working to transmit nerve impulses.) It appears that a genetic component may exist, but more research needs to be done. Although there are similarities with panic disorder, that condition involves spontaneous panic attacks unrelated to social triggers.

One treatment for social anxiety disorder is medication, particularly serotonin-specific reuptake inhibitors and benzodiazepines, especially the high-potency ones (see chapter 5). Cognitive-behavioral therapy has also proven quite effective, and, especially in combination with the right medicine, can result in a fairly high success rate. For some people, this disorder begins when they are young adults; others say that they've had the problem of excessive shyness for as long as they can remember. Some will avoid such seemingly simple acts as signing something in front of another person because of the fear that their hand might shake. Affected persons often have difficulty in dealing with store clerks, for example, and with going to public places such as restaurants. They often complain that, when they are around other people, they can't think, talk, or, if trying to eat in a public place, swallow. Sometimes nausea or other gastrointestinal discomfort occurs. Individuals may have trouble with blushing, perspiring too much, trembling, or other visible signs of anxiety, and, of course, this adds to their sense of embarrassment, thereby intensifying the problem. Estimates are that several million people in the United States experience this disorder each year.

Specific Phobia

This anxiety disorder, formerly called simple phobia, involves fear of a specific, circumscribed object or situation. Categories include fear of animals, of the natural environment, and of events involving blood, injections, or injuries. These fears interfere with the patients' ability to function socially or at work. Because of the circumscribed nature of the focus of anxiety, behavioral approaches alone work better than in many other conditions, where medications are all but essential. Treatment often involves gradual desensitization to the anxiety-provoking object or situation, sometimes with the aid of medication. These phobias include acrophobia (fear of heights), ailurophobia (fear of cats), amaxophobia (fear of vehicles or driving), arachnophobia (fear of spiders), brontophobia (fear of thunder), carcinophobia (fear of cancer), claustrophobia (fear of enclosed spaces or confinement), cynophobia (fear of dogs), entomophobia (fear of insects), musophobia (fear of mice), mysophobia (fear of dirt or germs), nyctophobia (fear of darkness or night), ophidiophobia (fear of snakes), pnigophobia (fear of choking), siderodromophobia (fear of trains), stygiophobia (fear of hell), thanatophobia (fear of death), and xenophobia (fear of strangers).

Depression

Although depression is usually referred to as a mood disorder, rather than an anxiety disorder, discussion of the condition is relevant here because there is a great deal of overlap in the symptoms of the two kinds of disorders (panic attacks can, in fact, be part of depression) and because antidepressant medication, for biochemical reasons, is one of the mainstays of treatment for panic disorder.

A major depressive episode is characterized either by the onset of a depressed mood or by a loss of pleasure or involvement in the things which used to interest the patient. Persons suffering from depression also frequently have some combination of other difficulties. They may have trouble with appetite disturbance, at some times losing weight and at others trying to console themselves by eating more and thus gaining. Sleep disturbance is also common; patients may have insomnia or a disarranged sleep cycle so that they sleep most of the day. People with this disorder often complain of easy fatigability and general loss of energy, along with difficulty concentrating.

They may have recurring thoughts of loss or death, perhaps of suicide. (Suicidal tendencies are not associated only with depression; they can occur in other psychiatric disorders, such as panic disorder and schizophrenia.) The depressed individual frequently shows what is known as psychomotor retardation, which involves a visible tendency to move and go about activities slowly. Patients often say that they have feelings of worthlessness, with an exaggerated sense of guilt; they sometimes become delusional and begin to think that they have been "condemned" because of some imagined transgression. Depression can become so severe that patients begin to hallucinate, hearing imaginary voices that typically make negative remarks about them.

Other Psychiatric Disorders

Although this book does not deal directly with certain of the psychiatric disorders, there is great similarity in symptoms between these and anxiety disorders, sometimes resulting in confusion as to which condition is involved.

Schizophrenia

Most psychiatrists consider schizophrenia to be a prototype example of the thought disorders, i.e., those in which the primary disturbance is in the processing and/or content of the patients' thoughts. Typically the symptoms of schizophrenia involve problems in perceiving reality and in integrating thoughts so as to cope with it. Frequently patients have hallucinations and delusions, and they often have trouble distinguishing metaphoric material from literal truth and vice versa. Persons with this disorder have difficulty understanding the interplay between thoughts and feelings and with subtleties of meaning that others understand intuitively. Most people recognize the impossibility of directly influencing the thoughts in another person's mind or of another person's thoughts being directly transmitted into their heads. Many individuals with schizophrenia have trouble with so fundamental a concept, however. They frequently misunderstand figures of speech, because they are operating at the wrong level of abstraction. If, for example, they find some situation to be "confining" in a figurative sense, they will often get the mistaken idea that they are literally imprisoned, or, if any sort of disagreement or controversy is going on, they may think that an actual conspiracy against them is under way. They also tend to confuse human attributes with those of inanimate objects, perhaps believing, for example, that a radio or television is talking directly to or about them or that voices are coming out of an air conditioner.

Schizophrenia, which was originally referred to as dementia praecox (precocious dementia) is not, in fact, a dementia, although at times it can be even more disabling. It typically first appears in the early decades of a person's life (hence "precocious"), and involves a deterioration of the individual's prior level of psychological and social adaptation, so that he or she never gets completely back to baseline. Schizophrenia generates a great deal of anxiety, and panic attacks can occur. Often the anxiety seems related to symptoms of paranoia, but sometimes it may involve a person's general feeling that his or her whole reality-system is coming unraveled.

Catatonia, often seen in schizophrenia, is a disorder in which patients become immobile or hyperactive in a way unrelated to reality-based objectives (for example, running aimlessly around the room or repeating the same phrase over and over). Once thought to occur only in schizophrenia, catatonia is commonly present in many disorders, especially the mood disorders.

Disorders of Mood Instability

Another group of psychiatric disorders is characterized by prominent mood swings. The prototype for this group is bipolar disorder, which used to be called manic-depression. The wide mood swings experienced by people who have this disorder involve alternating manic and depressive episodes, which interfere greatly with their lives. One of the mainstays in the treatment of mood instability disorders is a class of medications intended to counteract this tendency; the primary ones are lithium, carbamazepine (Tegretol), valproic acid (Depakote), clonazepam (Klonopin), and gabapentin (Neurontin). All of these except for lithium originally proved helpful as anticonvulsants, and there seems to exist at least some overlap between the mood instability disorders and seizure disorders such as epilepsy. Sometimes symptoms don't add up to full-blown bipolar disorder, but involve varying degrees of mood instability, such as disorders involving rapid-cycling, in which mood swings can occur over the course of just a few hours or days rather than of several weeks. Many of these rapid-cycling disorders tend to respond less well to lithium than does bipolar disorder. Also, some patients with rapid-cycling disorders have symptoms that seem aggravated by certain of the antidepressant medications, so adjustments must be made.

Attention-Deficit Hyperactivity Disorder (ADHD)

Although many consider this to be a childhood psychiatric disorder, its symptoms and social repercussions often persist well into adulthood. Sometimes those who have it are still suffering in later life from their lack of academic achievement in school and from a lingering sense of inferiority, since they always had trouble "fitting in." The onset of the disorder occurs before a child reaches the age of seven, and involves a disturbance that persists, by definition, for at least six months, with varying symptoms of restlessness, easy distractibility, and a tendency toward impulsive behavior. The condition has in the past gone by several names, including "minimal brain dysfunction." The general consensus has been that this disorder represents, at least in part, some sort of subtle neurological problem, but further investigation needs to be done into the specific nature of the dysfunction.

Related Physical Disorders

Mitral Valve Prolapse

Mitral valve prolapse is a disorder of one of the valves of the heart, and can be associated with a number of diseases, including thyroid disturbances, muscular dystrophy, and sickle cell disease, but it is also frequently found in panic disorder for reasons that are not completely clear. The mitral valve is found between the two chambers on the left side of the heart. For some reason, in this disorder, the leaflets of the valve give way when the heart pumps. Many people do not have symptoms, but when symptoms do occur, they frequently overlap with those of panic disorder. Patients often complain of fatigue and dizziness, shortness of breath, heart palpitations, and chest pain. Sometimes the doctor is able to hear a characteristic click-like murmur with the stethoscope, but other tests, such as electrocardiogram or echocardiogram, may be needed to confirm what's going on. Some patients who have this disorder may require antibiotics before such procedures as dental surgery to keep bacteria away from the damaged valve (endocarditis), and some may be advised to avoid competitive sports to prevent further damage to the valve. Heart medications known as beta blockers can sometimes block mitral valve-related symptoms in cases of panic disorder, but it helps to get the panic disorder under control, since the two syndromes seem to feed off each other in a vicious cycle, with the panic attacks bringing on more symptoms of mitral valve prolapse and the symptoms of the mitral valve problem bringing on more symptoms of panic disorder.

Headaches

Headaches occur frequently in people who are anxious, panicky, or depressed. Doctors generally try to specify these maladies as being either tension headaches or vascular headaches, but the truth is that the two types overlap, and so do the treatments for them. Often the physician will suggest nonsteroidal anti-inflammatory medications (NSAIDs, such as aspirin, ibuprofen, or naproxen), acetaminophen, and/or behavioral remedies. Prescription medications are also used; these include psychotropic medicines, beta blockers, ergot preparations, and sumatriptan (Imitrex, which stimulates one of the serotonin receptor subtypes). Sometimes doctors feel it necessary to use narcotics temporarily, but these tend to work better in the short term, and they come with the potential for habituation. Among the vascular headaches, the "classic migraine" has a warning prodrome, which can involve strange visual disturbances, before the onset of the headache itself, but many migraine headaches are "common migraines" and do not include prodromal symptoms.

Irritable Bowel Syndrome

Another of the general medical conditions that those with anxiety disorders frequently face is irritable bowel syndrome, a condition that has been known in the past as spastic colon and mucous colitis. Various parts of the bowel tend to react in different ways to stress, and often when there is a great deal of emotional stress they don't work in harmony. One part of the bowel may be trying to hurry contents along while another part is trying to slow things down, and the conflict is felt by the patient. Also, the bowel tends to get hypersensitive to pressure from gas, which adds to the problem. Constipation may alternate with diarrhea. Some patients become intolerant of certain foods, such as coffee, tea, citrus fruit, wheat products, or dairy products. Often this syndrome crops up at times of emotional stress, frequently coexisting with panic disorder. Mealtimes can be difficult, since eating often triggers symptoms. Those affected frequently complain of bloating and nausea, in addition to symptoms more often related to panic disorder, such as headache and fatigue. Patients' concerns about gastrointestinal symptoms gradually increase the general level of anxiety, contributing to overall stress and a tendency for panic disorder to be exacerbated. Determining that the patient has irritable bowel syndrome usually involves eliminating other possibilities. Since the condition's symptoms tend to be so nonspecific, a careful doctor will often have to perform a number of examinations and tests to ensure that something more serious is not being missed. A discerning physician, however, will pay attention to the patient's emotional situation as well.

After general medical problems are ruled out, the functional nature of the disorder calls for supportive treatment. In particular, it's helpful if psychiatric problems can be brought under control, since they often contribute to the problem, or, in fact, may be driving it. The symptoms of this disorder can be so variable and inconsistent that patients often end up seeing many doctors and having numereous tests so that all concerned can be reassured. Dietary changes may be as helpful as medications, and patients also often benefit from psychotherapy and simple reassurance.

3. Pictures of the Mind

The *Diagnostic and Statistical Manual of Mental Disorders*, published by the American Psychiatric Association, serves as a sort of Bible among mental health professionals. It first defined panic disorder as a distinct disorder, along with agoraphobia, in the third edition (*DSM III*), which was published in 1980. People may wonder whether a diagnosis is particularly important or is just a question of semantics. The main reason for putting so much time and effort into establishing diagnoses for different clusters of symptoms is that they are best treated in different ways. Psychiatrists may treat panic disorder one way and panic disorder with agoraphobia slightly differently. Generalized anxiety disorder has a different treatment from that of panic disorder or specific phobias. Psychiatrists have debated for many years the question of whether these disorders are genetic in nature or whether they represent a learned response—the "nature versus nurture" argument. In most circles the consensus is that they represent, for the most part, a combination of influences. It is apparent that a genetic component exists in these disorders, because statistically valid studies show that there is a tendency for certain of them to run in families in a manner inconsistent with simple learning. Numerous studies, such as those involving siblings separated at birth, have indicated that most psychiatric disturbances include some degree of genetic predisposition. It would be unrealistic, however, to believe that the circumstances in people's lives have no bearing on their emotional states when the evidence is to the contrary; hence the current philosophical compromise seems to be the best conclusion.

Psychiatry has gone through many phases regarding this question. Although recent approaches have stressed the biological component, at the beginning of the twentieth century a great deal of emphasis was placed on the learned aspects of personality (much of the philosophy for which still seems valid). One of the reasons was that in earlier days there was little in the way of medication available for the treatment of any of these disorders. Thus, the natural tendency was to emphasize areas amenable to treatment, namely those of a learned nature. Psychotherapy often lasted a very long time, with great effort made to uncover events in a person's past that would explain symptoms. It was believed that if such events could be discovered and addressed in psychotherapy, then the emotional energy tied up in them would diminish, or at the least better coping skills could be developed. This method of therapy continues to prove effective in some cases, but it's hard to achieve success when a biological, genetic influence is contributing heavily to the symptoms.

A fable that is usually told to second-year medical students when they are approaching the clinical part of their studies (that is, dealing with actual patients) is about six blind men asked to describe an elephant. These observers, positioned at various points around the animal, naturally come up with six different impressions; based on whether they are feeling the elephant's leg, trunk, tusk, ear, tail, or side, they think that they are confronting the trunk of a tree, a fire hose, a spear, a piece of cloth, a rope, or the wall of a house—all reasonable conclusions based on the limited information presented to them and given their restricted ability to observe. This is analogous to the study of medicine in general and to the study of psychiatry in particular, since, in many ways, it's difficult to see clearly the objects of study—namely thoughts, emotions, and patterns of behavior. Many well-meaning people see problems from different angles and make use of various terminologies, all of them attempting to describe and influence the same phenomena and all coming away with distinct impressions and approaches. Every so often the American Psychiatric Association comes out with a new and improved

Diagnostic and Statistical Manual, which a few years later becomes obsolete. Despite the inevitable obsolescence, however, the *DSM* continues to represent the best available estimate of the mysterious subjects of our attentions. The most we can do is to make use of current research in order to give our patients the best care available.

Personality is one of the more elusive concepts in psychiatry, even though people have been talking about its significance since at least the fourth century b.c.e. Hippocrates, for example, observed that persons with long-standing maladaptive personality traits were prone to melancholia, and Democritus apparently quipped at one point that if the body should ever try to take legal action against the soul for ill treatment, it would have a solid case.

The personality consists of persistent and ubiquitous habits pertaining to the way in which one deals with the environment and including the degree to which one can understand the motivations and feelings of other people (empathy). Sometimes the term "personality" is used interchangeably with "character" and "temperament"; originally, however, the meanings differed from each other somewhat. "Character" comes from a Greek word for an instrument used for engraving, and implies that a personality has distinctive features, particularly as acquired through developmental processes and life experiences. The word "temperament," however, refers primarily to those biological predispositions that help to shape the personality. Back in medieval times, doctors referred to specific types of temperament: melancholic (sad), choleric (irritable), sanguine (optimistic), and phlegmatic (apathetic). These temperaments were supposedly related to the four "bodily humors," which harkened back to the Greeks' early theory about the role allegedly played by physiology. (Each of the temperament types would be the result of the influence of, respectively, black bile, yellow bile, blood, or phlegm.) Interestingly, after going through a phase early in the twentieth century in which people's psychological status was considered to be almost entirely the result of environment and learning, psychiatry has come full circle, in a roundabout way, and is now maintaining that much is dependent on neurotransmitters.

In any event, the combination of character and temperament results in what is known as "personality," which is of interest here because of the interaction of personality, environment, and biology in the bringing about of panic disorder. David Shapiro's classic study *Neurotic Styles* gives an excellent overview of four different types of personality. In the case of each type, the emotional conflicts and stress present in varying situations increase the person's general level of anxiety and move him or her closer to panic (e.g., the obsessive-compulsive type loses control over the details in life, the hysterical type is no longer the center of attention, or the paranoid type gets cornered by people or things that seem to be enemies). In his book *Adaptation to Life*, George Vaillant examines various coping mechanisms, explaining how they either help a person adapt to the changes in life, create added distress farther down the road, or cause a breakdown of the individual's social support network. He characterizes the mechanisms that work best as "mature" defenses (i.e., coping tactics); those slightly less adaptive are called the "neurotic" defenses (see "repression" in glossary), followed by the "immature" defenses, and then, least adaptively, by the "psychotic" defenses. The mature defenses involve such personality traits as a sense of humor and altruism, as well as the ability to rechannel unacceptable impulses into more acceptable alternative endeavors that still provide an emotional outlet for the impulses (sublimation). At the other end of the spectrum are the tendencies in which reality is badly distorted, including delusions and denial; these provide poor solutions to life's problems and are more common in the chronic, debilitating psychiatric disorders such as schizophrenia and drug dependency. Many of these less adaptive coping mechanisms are normally found in children under a certain age, but in psychiatric disorders the patients either don't grow out of them or regress to the stage of using them again, abandoning the more mature and functional defenses.

The Biopsychosocial Model

Psychiatry's approach to problems has recently been informed by the so-called biopsychosocial model. The field of medicine has traditionally been dominated by what is known as the biomedical model, which involves the approach that has characterized Western science for many years, and is still very much in evidence in many nonpsychiatric areas today. According to the biomedical model, a doctor relieves a patient of pain and suffering that an illness or disease has brought about. The problem with this model, especially in the psychiatric area, is that it takes into consideration only part of the whole picture, and many of the psychological and social variables are forgotten in the process, leaving out an important dimension in our understanding which the biopsychosocial model more reliably delivers; in such an appoach the biological, intrapsychic, and social aspects are considered together in a manner that takes the whole system into account. It is rare in the practice of psychiatry to see a patient whose problems appear to be purely biological; usually there is some cognitive, emotional, or behavioral habit, often unconscious, that the patient is acting in response to, and which is frequently traceable by considering the person's social history. Just as commonly, the doctor finds many stressors in the patient's current situation that are contributing significantly to his or her symptoms. The mind functions at the interface between the biological, psychological, and social areas, and if the broader picture is not considered, doctors often find themselves using medication with patients whose symptoms don't respond to a purely biomedical approach.

4. Who Gets Anxiety Disorders?

It's estimated that in the United States somewhere between three and six million people will have panic disorder at some point in their lives. Ongoing research is attempting to isolate specific genetic factors that contribute to panic disorder and the other anxiety disorders. It is fairly clear that at least some of the anxiety disorders occur with greater-than-average frequency among close relatives than in the remainder of the population. Details, however, are far from being completely understood. Close relatives of patients suffering from panic disorder, for example, have about a four-to-seven-times greater chance of getting panic disorder than in the population at large, and studies of identical twins tend to support the impression that there is a clear genetic component. Most studies of generalized anxiety disorder, however, show inconsistent family tendencies.

Often patients suffering from panic disorder can identify their first attack as having happened at a time of particularly high stress in their lives, and they and their doctors have to reconstruct the list of stressors retrospectively. It is common for sufferers of panic disorder not to be cognizant of just how much stress has been gradually accumulating, and it is also the case that many people expect to be able to go emotionally unscathed through major life changes, such as divorce, moving, the death of a loved one, medical problems, or job-related difficulties.

Emotional stress caused by situations that interfere with normal emotional and physiological equilibrium is a major contributing factor to psychiatric illnesses, including the anxiety disorders. Stress can affect people in subtle psychological, physical, and behavioral ways, as well as in interpersonal patterns of communication (or lack of communication) and does not necessarily result in overt psychiatric syndromes. Sometimes the degree of stress felt by patients is influenced by prior sensitization (or desensitization) to certain situations. Psychological symptoms include restlessness, worry, and feelings of nervous tension, along with moodiness, low motivation, and low levels of energy. Stress is often accompanied by sleep and appetite disturbance and sometimes by muscle tension (causing various kinds of aches and pains), pacing, and grinding of the teeth (bruxism). Stress is one of the major contributing factors in the development of temporomandibular joint (TMJ) syndrome. Physiological effects include the excessive release into the bloodstream of certain naturally occurring chemicals from various organs, in particular the adrenal glands. These glands, located near the kidneys, have a variety of functions. During times of stress they are stimulated to produce extra amounts of adrenaline and cortisol. Both of these chemicals have a number of physiological actions, many of which help the organism to survive, but long-term excessive production can be quite detrimental. Overproduction can, for instance, contribute to an increased incidence of cardiovascular disease and a general decrease in the body's immune response. Stress also contributes to elevated blood pressure and to peptic ulcer disease.

The impact of stress on patients can be decreased by the adjustment of their coping skills through psychotherapy. People often tend to be inflexible in dealing with life's vicissitudes, and many of their habits are automatic, with individuals being unconscious of them. Professionals are not immune to the effects of stress; in fact, the term "burnout" seems particularly suited to those who have high expectations for themselves or are in positions of responsibility.

Health-sustaining habits, such as proper exercise, relaxation, and diet, can also minimize the impact of stress, as does the ability to pace oneself. Some people don't realize that there are limitations as to how much stress they can handle in meeting continual deadlines. It may be a cliché, but it's also true: many of us get too caught up in the "rat race" of modern life to pursue the satisfactions afforded by family, friends, nature, the arts, humor, and spirituality. People become trapped on a treadmill partly of their own making, and may not even be aware of the pace of their lives. In our rapidly changing world, information and paradigm shifts come at us with overwhelming speed, so that the problem is not one of getting information but of what to do with it.

Another contributing factor in the development of syndromes similar to panic disorder is the tendency to over-indulge in caffeine or alcohol. It is quite common for people misguidedly to self-medicate with alcohol, only to find that the apparent benefits are short-lived and quickly lead to an increase in the sensations of panic. Nicotine withdrawal is frequently associated with symptoms of anxiety, but often the heart rate is decreased, in contrast to the increase usually associated with anxiety attacks. Problems can result from the use of certain medications, including decongestants and medications for treating asthma such as theophylline or aminophylline, which are closely related chemically to caffeine. Many diet pills are stimulants and can contribute to the onset of panic attacks. Prednisone, which is used to treat such illnesses as asthma, rheumatoid arthritis, and lupus, can also be a factor in this syndrome. Some medical conditions, such as hyperthyroidism, can closely mimic the symptoms of panic disorder.

Persons susceptible to panic also tend to get what is known as "air hunger." For unclear reasons, anxious people often get the notion that they are not getting enough air, so they start to breathe more rapidly, thus altering their blood chemistry (making it more alkaline), which causes them to feel even more anxious. This cycle of hyperventilation can result in a panic attack.

Chemical changes in the body clearly contribute to the occurrence of panic attacks. One of the tests used to diagnose panic disorder is the lactate infusion test, in which a physician injects lactic acid (lactate) intravenously, often precipitating a panic attack in individuals with panic disorder.

The Nervous System

Let us look more closely at what researchers believe is happening in the brain—what causes one nerve cell to transmit its information to the next one, thus affecting patients' moods. The brain is filled with bundles of nerve fibers that travel predictably with certain anatomical connections and are also linked to chemicals called neurotransmitters that allow the nerve cells to communicate with each other. Panic disorder, as well as many other psychiatric conditions, is influenced by some disturbance in these neurochemical and neuroanatomical systems. One of the main areas involving the emotions is the limbic system, where many of the neurotransmitters governing emotions and their corresponding nerve pathways are at work (fig. 4.1).

The human brain is composed of several parts, each having different functions. The anatomy of the nervous system (neuroanatomy) can be studied during an autopsy, but the function of the nervous system is trickier to research. Sometimes information can be gathered by studying patients who have had strokes or injuries to specific areas of the brain; it is possible to determine what functions have become deficient and then to verify the areas involved through various imaging studies (discussed later in this chapter) or in an autopsy. Generalizations regarding neural function may be made through research on similar areas in animal brains, but extrapolating those results to humans can sometimes be misleading.

The cortex contains the nerve cell bodies that we usually associate with higher mental functions. It supports the highest

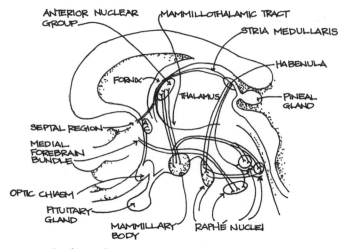

FIG. 4.I. Limbic pathways.

level of sensation and perception, and is associated with memory, personality, and thinking. Just under this area are nerve fibers. The part of the brain known as the thalamus represents an older, i.e., more "reptilian," site for sensory integration. Although it plays a more prominent role in lower animals, in humans it sends much sensory information to the cortex. Nearby are various parts of the brain called the basal ganglia, which also represent an older part of the brain, and are primarily associated with an older system of motor coordination, in contrast to the largely sensory-relay function of the thalamus. Below these are the midbrain, pons, and medulla, which contain ascending and descending nerve fibers (i.e., from body to brain and from brain to body), as well as clusters of nerve cells called nuclei. The cerebellum helps to integrate muscle coordination and tone, and is located near the pons on the backside of the brainstem. The whole apparatus ends up in the spinal cord (fig. 4.2).

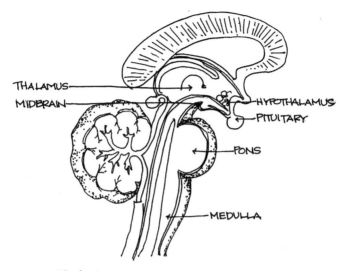

FIG. 4.2. The brainstem.

The Autonomic Nervous System

There has been much talk recently about right brain functions versus left brain functions, but the study of the newer parts of the brain versus the older parts is at least equally important. The functions of many of the physically lower parts of the brain are less conscious and more primitive. A part of the nervous system that operates largely unconsciously and has to do with the regulation of the internal organs and the skin is known as the autonomic nervous system (since it seems to have a mind of its own). In fact, however, its workings tie in closely with the emotions, and the other mental functions affect it heavily. Nerve impulses proceed from the internal organs to the brain and from the brain back to the internal organs constantly, whether someone is asleep or awake, for the most part without the person's awareness. The two main parts of the autonomic nervous system are the sympathetic and parasympathetic nervous systems, and most of the internal organs send and receive signals from both of these. The two parts often act antagonistically, with their activity coordinated by the brain. The sympathetic nervous system acts to dilate the pupils of the eyes, reduce the secretion of the salivary glands, increase the production of sweat, enlarge the air passages in the lungs, elevate the heartbeat, inhibit gastrointestinal activity, stimulate the release of adrenaline (epinephrine) by the adrenal glands, and constrict blood vessels in the trunk and extremities— in other words, it governs much of the standard physiology involved in the "fight or flight" response. For the most part, sympathetic nerve impulses cause the ultimate release of norepinephrine. (Epinephrine, however, eventually gets released in the adrenal medulla, and acetylcholine is released at sweat glands and certain skeletal muscle fibers.) The parasympathetic nervous system acts in the opposite way, constricting the pupils, causing the tear glands to secrete tears, activating the salivary glands, constricting the air passages in the lungs, decreasing the activity of the heart, activating the gastrointestinal tract, and emptying the bladder—in short, assisting in the digestion of food and other functions after the need to fight or flee is over. (The activity of both of these systems are needed during sex, with the parasympathetic nervous system causing the dilation of blood vessels in the sex organs and erection in the male and the sympathetic nervous system causing ejaculation.) Parasympathetic nerve impulses cause the ultimate release of acetylcholine or a closely related substance; medications said to be "anticholinergic" tend to be antagonistic to this system (fig. 4.3).

These two parts of the autonomic nervous system tie in closely with the emotions and greatly affect the function of internal organs, thereby contributing to disorders such as irritable bowel syndrome and mitral valve prolapse (see chapter 2).

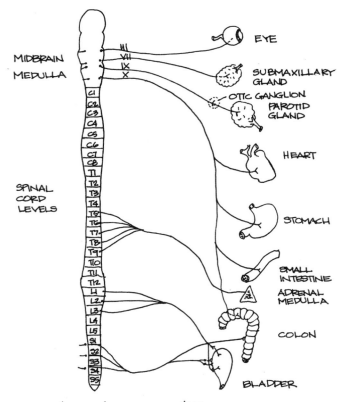

FIG. 4.3. Autonomic nerve connections.

Polarization, Depolarization, and Nerve Impulses

The nerve pathways in the brain are very complicated. The flow of ions (that is, charged particles) through the membranes of these nerve cells contributes, in large part, to the activity of these pathways, and the opening and closing of ion channels in the membranes has a great deal to do with the ability of the ions to flow in and out of the cells. For example, typically, there is a greater concentration of sodium, calcium, and chloride ions outside the nerve cells than inside them, where the concentration of potassium is higher. A nerve cell (neuron) that is at rest (not firing) tends to be polarized; that is, the outside of the cell has a slightly positive electrical charge compared to inside the cell membrane. When the nerve cell fires, often caused by an adjacent cell firing, it depolarizes, or loses this voltage charge across the cell membrane. Much of the tendency for these cells to be polarized at rest comes from the action of ion pumps, structures in the cell membranes that pump ions into or out of the cells; e.g., the sodium pump pushes sodium ions out of the cells, these positive ions helping to keep the resting cell electrically positive on the outside. A large portion of the activity of these nerve cells has to do with the opening and closing of ion channels, principally those regulating the flow of positively charged sodium, potassium, and calcium ions and negatively charged chloride ions. In other words, most of the activity of the brain is governed chemically, and even minor changes in this chemistry can have effects on thoughts and emotions.

Once electrical and chemical events cause the nerve cell's polarization to be reduced a certain amount, the cell reaches a spike threshold, at which point the cell fires. The opening of sodium or calcium channels tends to depolarize the cell membrane, because these ions try to enter the cell with their positive charge. Then the opening of potassium or chloride channels shortly after the spike threshold drives the voltage inside the cell back even farther in the negative direction, for a brief period, than before the depolarization process started. This is called hyperpolarization. After a brief period of time, the hyperpolarization goes away, and the cell once again returns to its previous resting voltage.

Much of the regulation of these ion channels and the firing of various nerve cells is a result of the activity of chemicals known as neurotransmitters. Currently, most researchers designate nine different neurotransmitters. The first group is made up of chemicals called amines, and includes serotonin, norepinephrine, dopamine, and acetylcholine. The second group consists of certain amino acids, and includes gamma-amino butyric acid (GABA), glycine, L-glutamic acid, and L-aspartic acid. The third group is composed of peptides, which are chemically similar to proteins but with shorter chains. The main focus of research in this group is a chemical called substance P, which was discovered several decades ago and has recently been getting much attention (see chapter 6).

Researchers use several approaches to study the effects of neurotransmitter chemicals on nerve cells. One of these is to apply the neurotransmitter directly to the nerve cell from some source outside the brain. Another is to stimulate nerve pathways that connect to the cell being studied so that the neurotransmitter is increased in concentration near the cell. Each of these methods has advantages and disadvantages. Just because a nerve cell responds in a certain way to a neuro-transmitter under experimental conditions doesn't necessarily mean that the same neurotransmitter would actually affect it in the brain in real life. It's also hard to isolate a nerve cell and get meaningful information, because in a real brain numerous unpredictable, unanticipated factors are influen-tial. Just to make things a bit more complicated, nerve cells appear to have two main types of neurotransmitter receptors that interact with the ion channels. These are called ligand-gated channels and G-protein-coupled receptors. Ligand-gated channels involve the direct attachment of the neuro-transmitter to a chunk of the protein that is part of the ion channel itself. The G-protein-coupled receptors are more complex, involving a receptor site that is not in direct contact with the ion channel, but which activates a receptor protein. Part of this, in turn, activates either the ion channel or an intracellular second messenger system, which then activates the ion channel. This second messenger system serves as an intermediary between a neurotransmitter (or hormone) and the ultimate ion channel target, and usually involves the chemicals cyclic adenosine monophosphate (cAMP), cyclic guanosine monophosphate (cGMP), calcium, or metabolites of phosphatidylinositol. Researchers are now starting to categorize neurotransmitters based on what receptor subtype they react with and what particular ion system they activate (i.e., sodium, potassium, chloride, or calcium).

The actions of most psychotropic medicines can be linked in some fashion to one or more of the neurotransmitter receptor systems. For example, benzodiazepines are among the main types of antianxiety agents in clinical use today. The antianxiety activity of these medications seems related in particular to the GABA-A receptor. (There is also a GABA-B receptor that seems to be less intimately related to the psychotropic actions of the medication.) It seems that the GABA-A receptors primarily associate with chloride channels, letting GABA open them to the influx of chloride ions, thus making the interior of the cell even more negative (hyperpolarizing it) and generally inhibiting the cell's tendency to fire. GABA seems to be the most important inhibitory neurotransmitter in the brain, and, because its actions are so pervasive, it serves a great many functions, including those of an anticonvulsant and sleep-inducing nature. The effect of benzodiazepines on the GABA system shows a rapidity of action, and discontinuation can give withdrawal side effects. The combination of these two factors, along with the tendency for benzodiazepines to give some individuals a feeling of euphoria, means that this medication carries the potential for abuse and habituation. Because of the multiplicity of the medication's actions, rapid reduction in dosage or discontinuation of the benzodiazepines can cause an increase in anxiety and insomnia, and there have even been occasional reports of convulsions. Most of the medications pertaining to psychiatric disorders are in the group related to the G-protein-coupled receptors.

Knowing something about the antidotes to emotional disorders helps us understand more about the underlying

factors behind the disorders themselves. Among the antidepressants, the tricyclic antidepressants (TCAs), monoamine
oxidase inhibitors (MAOIs), and serotonin-specific reuptake
inhibitors (SSRIs) all tend to affect the actions and concentrations of serotonin and/or norepinephrine. Most of the
tricyclic antidepressants block the reuptake of serotonin or
norepinephrine or both, so that their concentrations build up
at the communication points between nerve cells (synapses).

The TCAs are referred to as "tricyclic" because of their
molecular structure, which contains three rings. Researchers
discovered TCAs in the same period of time when they were
working with other three-ringed molecules that turned out to
be effective in the treatment of schizophrenia, such as chlorpromazine (widely known by the trade name Thorazine). The
tricyclic antidepressants turned out to be less than effective
when used against symptoms of psychosis, as in schizophrenia, and their significance in the treatment of depression
and panic disorder was nearly missed. Astute researchers,
however, noticed that patients who were also depressed began
to show fewer symptoms of that condition when they were
taking these medications—thus the discovery of this entire
group of antidepressants and antipanic agents.

Monoamine oxidase inhibitors cause an increase in the
amount of serotonin and norepinephrine in the synapses
between nerve cells. Because these medications have such
an effect on norepinephrine, which in turn affects blood
pressure, attention should be paid to the blood pressure of
a patient using MAOIs. This new class of antidepressant and
antipanic medication was discovered accidentally when researchers testing an antituberculous drug noticed that patients
who were also depressed began to show improvement in the
symptoms of that disorder.

Serotonin-specific reuptake inhibitors differ from tricyclic
antidepressants in several ways, despite some superficial
similarities. They don't seem to have much effect on nore-
pinephrin, and they have fewer in general anticholinergic

features. Part of the impetus for research on SSRIs was the bothersome side effects, many of them anticholinergic in nature, which patients experienced when taking TCAs. Researchers stumbled onto something that had so little effect on norepinephrine that they thought at first that it wouldn't be very strong against depression, but the results of their studies showed otherwise. These agents were found to be quite effective against depression and panic disorder, as well as against obsessive-compulsive disorder, which the tricyclic antidepressants (with the notable exception of clomipramine) didn't much affect.

The Neurotransmitter Receptor Hypothesis of Antidepressant Action

A realistic explanation of the antidepressant and antipanic action of antidepressant medications must take into account the well-recognized delay, usually two to three weeks, from the time patients begin a therapeutic dosage of the medication until they feel significant relief from their target symptoms. The fact is that no one has yet managed to come up with a completely adequate theory as to how psychotropic medications work. We know from numerous empirical studies that antidepressant medications are helpful in treating depression and panic disorder, that benzodiazepines are effective in treating anxiety, that neuroleptics work in the treatment of psychosis, and that lithium and several other agents are valuable in treating the mood swings of bipolar disorder, but we still don't know exactly what is going on in the brain.

The most often quoted theory, one that provides the best overall explanation so far and that seems consistent with most of the raw data accumulated from research, is referred to as the neurotransmitter receptor hypothesis of antidepressant action. According to this theory, something is wrong with the receptors on certain of the nerve cells that adjust

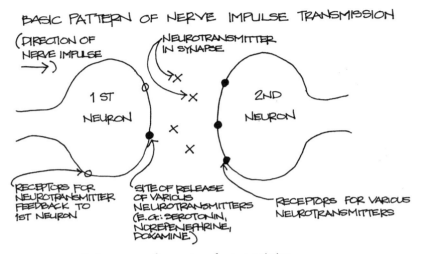

BASIC PATTERN OF NERVE IMPULSE TRANSMISSION

(DIRECTION OF NERVE IMPULSE ⟶)

NEUROTRANSMITTER IN SYNAPSE

1 ST NEURON

2ND NEURON

RECEPTORS FOR NEUROTRANSMITTER FEEDBACK TO 1ST NEURON

SITE OF RELEASE OF VARIOUS NEUROTRANSMITTERS (E.G.: SEROTONIN, NOREPENEPHRINE, DOXAMINE.)

RECEPTORS FOR VARIOUS NEUROTRANSMITTERS

FIG. 4.4. Basic pattern of nerve impulse transmission.

the person's mood, specifically nerve cells involving serotonin, norepinephrine, and/or dopamine (fig. 4.4). This is a modification of an earlier theory, known as the monoamine hypothesis, which is now considered by most to be overly simplistic; the idea was that the neurotransmitters were simply present in the synapses in subnormal concentrations, resulting in mood disturbance. What was supposed to have depleted these neurotransmitters was not completely clear, but it could have included a number of factors, such as heredity, stress, and drugs of various types. For example, certain drugs that depleted relevant neurotransmitters, such as reserpine (an old-fashioned medicine for treating high blood pressure), seemed to induce depression, while those that increased the concentration of the involved neurotransmitters, such as the MAOIs, tended to get rid of depression.

Further study has revealed, however, that it is not simply the concentration of the neurotransmitters in the synapses that is causing the problem, but also the concomitant increase in neurotransmitter receptor activity on the nerve cell that's receiving the message after the synapse (at the postsynaptic receptors; receptors located on the nerve cell before the synapses are presynaptic receptors). This is known as an up-regulation of the postsynaptic receptors. The neurotransmitter receptor hypothesis is linked in particular to this up-regulation of neurotransmitter receptor sites at that second nerve cell at the far end of the synapse, and the up-regulation seems closely related to depression. Why that might cause depression is not clear. (It may be that the receptors are "hungry" for more of the neurotransmitter, and are compensating for the neurotransmitter deficiency.) The general idea with most of the antidepressant medications is that they down-regulate these neurotransmitter receptor sites, which is what somehow makes them effective. The story vis-à-vis the development of panic disorder is more complicated still. One theory about the development of this disorder proposes that there is an initial increase in the concentration of norepinephrine, causing a compensatory down-regulation in the postsynaptic adrenergic receptors.

There is also a question as to whether or not the GABA-A receptor may be out of kilter in those with panic disorder, so that the patient feels a "need" for benzodiazepines to help stave off panic attacks. It's possible that some naturally occurring chemical is present in either too little or too great a concentration, interfering with the GABA receptor's activity so that the benzodiazepine is needed to compensate for it. Another biological theory regarding the development of panic disorder involves the notion of hypersensitivity to carbon dioxide; researchers have noted that affected persons tend to be unusually sensitive to this gas when it occurs in above-normal amounts. (This might also explain why panic disorder patients tend to feel short of breath during panic attacks.) Researchers have suggested that the brain may have some sort of "alarm system" that causes the patients to hyperventilate because they fear they are not getting enough air.

Another consideration is that certain subtle anatomical

differences are found in the brains of panic disorder patients, and these seem to be centered in the limbic areas of the brain (see chapter 6), which have a great deal to do with emotional function. The term "limbic lobe" does not actually refer to a lobe of the brain but to a number of structures that are intimately tied in with the emotions. A more correct term is "limbic system," since these structures seem linked together functionally. To be more specific, the limbic system involves certain areas of the brain, such as the hippocampus, parahippocampal gyrus, amygdala, hypothalamus, cingulate gyrus, fornix, mamillary bodies, and olfactory regions, as well as the septal area, dorsal raphé nuclei, and locus ceruleus. The limbic area was first designated by Paul Broca, the French anatomist, and researchers have since studied it in great detail, trying to shed light on its link to the emotions. The connection of the limbic system through the hypothalamus with the autonomic nervous system has led to its being called a "visceral brain." Much of the limbic system's function appears related to that part of the brain believed to be older, evolutionarily, than other parts. This paleocortex, or "old cortex," part of the brain involves much of the limbic system, and contributes heavily to our human qualities, since no matter how logical we may try to be, we are still alternately plagued by and blessed with emotions.

The exact role played by the limbic system continues to be a mystery, but researchers are beginning to shed some light on it. In 1937, Dr. James Papez proposed that the brain was employing a particular circuit (now known as the Papez circuit) that involved part of the limbic system, and suggested that these "older" parts of the brain were following predictable patterns, using this circuit, while interacting with the "newer" parts of the brain. He believed that the more sophisticated areas of the brain channel information into the more primitive and deeper structures through the cingulate gyrus. According to this theory, the information goes to the hippocampus and the amygdala, and then, by way of the fornices, through the

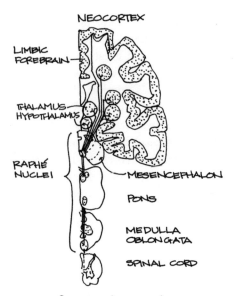

FIG. 4.5. Serotonergic connections.

mamillary bodies. From that point, it goes to the anterior thalamus, and ends up eventually returning to the cingulate gyrus. It now appears that this was an oversimplification of the emotional processes. Much of what goes on in the limbic system involves the neurotransmitters serotonin, norepinephrine, and dopamine, with a good part of their activity starting in the lower, more posterior, parts of the brain and ending up in the higher, more anterior, parts. Much of the serotonin, for example, originates in an area in and around the dorsal raphé nuclei, located in the midbrain, and much of their energy seems to be directed toward higher centers in the brain through a group of fibers (the medial forebrain bundle), ending up in the hippocampus, amygdala, and septal area, as well as in some other sites (fig. 4.5). Many of the noradrenergic pathways originate a bit farther back in the brain, in the pons and the medulla. Much of the norepinephrine there comes from an area in and around the locus ceruleus, or "dark blue place." Fibers arising in this area follow several different pathways in their journey toward higher centers in the brain. Some of them proceed through the medial forebrain bundle, as mentioned above, and end up innervating the hippocampus, amygdala, and septal area, as well as certain other sites, in a manner similar to the way serotonin works (fig. 4.6). Dopaminergic pathways start primarily in an area of the midbrain in and around the substantia nigra, or "black substance." They end up proceeding through several different pathways, including the mesolimbic pathway, which delivers dopamine to the amygdala, the septal area, and another structure called the nucleus accumbens (fig. 4.7).

The body synthesizes norepinephrine, dopamine, and serotonin from certain amino acids that come, in turn, from the metabolic breakdown of proteins. Norepinephrine and dopamine fall into a group of chemicals called catecholamines, which derive by one route or another from the amino acid L-phenylalanine. The L-phenylalanine converts to L-tyrosine,

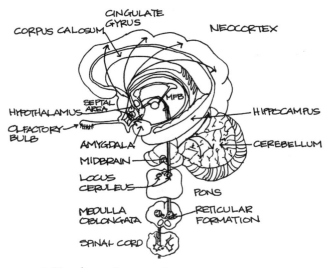

FIG. 4.6. Noradrenergic connections.

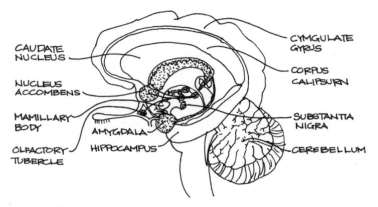

FIG. 4.7. Dopaminergic connections.

another amino acid, and then to L-DOPA, which ends up eventually as dopamine. Dopamine then undergoes a chemical change (hydroxylation), in which it is converted into norepinephrine. In the adrenal medulla, norepinephrine can change once again, this time into epinephrine (adrenaline). The thyroid hormones that help to regulate the body's rate of metabolism also derive indirectly from this same amino acid system by combining with iodine, then recombining to form thyroid hormones, such as L-thyroxin. Serotonin, on the other hand, derives from another amino acid, L-tryptophan, and is closely related to the melatonin bought in health food stores to promote sleep. Norepinephrine, dopamine, and serotonin all use the monoamine oxidase enzyme in their metabolic breakdown, so anything that affects the activity of monoamine oxidase affects the concentration of these three neurotransmitters.

From a research standpoint, the anatomy and function of these neurotransmitters shed important light on how psychotropic medications seem to work.

5. Treatment

Medications

Antidepressant medications and benzodiazepines are main-stays in the pharmacological treatment of panic disorder. As we have seen, antidepressant medications come in several different forms, including the older tricyclic antidepressants (TCAs), such as imipramine, amitriptyline, and doxepin, and monoamine oxidase inhibitors (MAOIs), such as phenelzine and tranylcypromine, as well as in more recently developed agents, including the serotonin-specific reuptake inhibitors (SSRIs), such as fluoxetine, sertraline, and paroxetine. These medications, with the exception of the benzodiazepines, generally take about two to three weeks to be fully effective. (Antipsychotic medications may be helpful, although they are used less commonly, as are medications for attention-deficit hyperactivity disorder.) One of the main reasons that family physicians and emergency room doctors end up referring patients to psychiatrists is that everybody gives up on the medicine before it's had a chance to work. Granted, there are few afflictions that give doctors and patients a greater sense of urgency in the need for relief than panic disorder, but it often pays off to wait; patients sometimes want to abandon an antidepressant they've been on for only one week. Another common reason for referral is that physicians are hesitant to recommend a high enough dosage of a type of medication they may not be used to prescribing.

Tricyclic Antidepressants (TCAs)

Tricyclic antidepressants have played an important part in the treatment of panic disorder for some time now. They include the medications imipramine (Tofranil), amitriptyline

(Elavil), desipramine (Norpramin), nortriptyline (Pamelor), and doxepin (Sinequan). These drugs are fairly safe, but they do have a number of limitations, primarily because of their side effects. The TCAs work by affecting the neurotransmitters serotonin and norepinephrine. Many complicated theories have been put forth to explain the mechanisms of the antidepressant and antipanic action of these medications, most involving the idea of alterations in the chemical concentrations of these neurotransmitters between nerve cells in the brain and the resulting changes in the function and structure of the same nerve cells. Much of the therapeutic effect seems to be related to the down-regulation of certain neurotransmitter receptor sites (see chapter 6). There has been some benefit derived, on occasion, from checking the chemical blood concentrations of certain of these TCAs, but, for the most part, clinicians are able to get by without doing so, basing dosage decisions on information as to usual therapeutic doses, relief of target symptoms (those which the medicine is specifically designed to alleviate), and emergent side effects.

Many of the side effects of these medications, e.g., dry mouth, blurred vision, and constipation, are related to what clinicians call the anticholinergic effects (see chapter 6). Although they are not considered habituating in the usual sense of the word, rapid discontinuation of TCAs (and other of the antidepressants) can, at times, lead to temporary flu-like withdrawal symptoms. These drugs can also cause certain cardiovascular conditions. Sometimes patients develop orthostatic hypotension, in which blood pressure does not equilibrate as fast as it would without the medication, so that individuals become lightheaded if they stand up too quickly. Users of TCAs sometimes notice that their heart rate has increased. These drugs can be particularly dangerous if an overdose is taken. Sometimes side effects are dependent on the dosage, and decreasing it (if that can be done without detracting from the therapeutic effect) may reduce such effects. In other cases, however, the side reactions are not related to dosage, and the medication has to be stopped if the situation becomes too bothersome for the patient. Patients often complain of side effects related to sexuality, such as decreased interest in sex or decreased ability to perform. Many antidepressants, and the TCAs in particular, cause weight gain. Another side effect reported by those using TCAs is a slight hand tremor, which some people find embarrassing. The range of these side reactions can limit the usefulness of the medications.

Monoamine Oxidase Inhibitors (MAOIs)

The MAOIs are quite effective for panic disorder, but their use is complicated. They inhibit an enzyme that helps, directly or indirectly, with the breakdown of certain neurotransmitters and hormones, such as norepinephrine, epinephrine, dopamine, and serotonin. The MAOIs include the medications phenelzine (Nardil), tranylcypromine (Parnate), and isocarboxazid (Marplan). Patients who take these medications must follow a special diet that requires them to avoid foods rich in a chemical called tyramine, which causes the release of norepinephrine. Such foods include a variety of prepared meat and dairy products, especially those involving aging, pickling, fermentation, or smoking, which means most cheeses, pickled herring, beer, wine (especially red wines), liver, yeast extract, dry sausage, broad beans, and yogurt. Patients also have to avoid many of the other antidepressant drugs and even certain over-the-counter preparations for colds and coughs, as well as medications for asthma, hay fever, and sinus problems, since many of them, when used together with MAOIs, can cause a dangerous buildup of norepinephrine concentration. Weight-reduction medicines, "pep pills," and the chemical L-tryptophan should not be taken. Any sort of narcotics or opioids can be dangerous when combined with MAOIs, and patients have to be careful about the use of caffeine, chocolate, and alcohol. The reason for such caution is the concern that the combination of tyramine-rich foods and MAOIs could cause a hypertensive crisis, which means that the blood pressure shoots up and is out of control; it is a medical emergency, and can sometimes be fatal. There is also a long list of prescription medicines that users of MAOIs have to avoid or use with great care. The MAOIs can cause hypotension (low blood pressure) as well, simply as a routine side effect. However, although many problems can occur, these medications are potent inhibitors of panic attacks.

Serotonin-Specific Reuptake Inhibitors (SSRIs)

Newer medications, as mentioned above, include the serotonin-specific reuptake inhibitors, which affect serotonin, one of the neurotransmitters in the brain, almost exclusively. Serotonin is a major neurotransmitter in the limbic system, and disturbances in its function seem closely related to symptoms of depression and panic disorder. The first of these drugs introduced in the United States was fluoxetine (Prozac), with sertraline (Zoloft), paroxetine (Paxil), fluvoxamine (Luvox), and citalopram (Celexa) soon following. These medicines are potent reuptake inhibitors in serotonergic systems presynaptically; they decrease the amount of serotonin reabsorbed into the transmitting nerve cell, thus making more of it available in the synapse, the region between the two nerve cells. This results in down-regulation of serotonin receptors on certain nerve cells postsynaptically; that is, the level of receiving activity of the nerve cell receiving the transmission is diminished. This seems, in turn, to bear a close relationship to antidepressant and antipanic actions.

The SSRIs tend to have fewer side effects than the older antidepressants, but some do occur. One problem involves sexual dysfunction. Many patients, men and women alike, who take these medicines experience a general lack of interest in sex and have difficulty reaching climax; men often have trouble achieving erection. People may be embarrassed about mentioning such problems unless the doctor specifically asks. These difficulties are temporary, disappearing when the patients stop the medications, but can cause significant distress until then. Sometimes patients complain that for the first day or two of taking SSRIs they feel a bit edgy, and they may have insomnia if they take the medicine too close to bedtime. Some also notice looseness of stools. But many of the difficulties, such as dry mouth, symptoms of orthostatic hypotension, blurred vision, and constipation, which are so often experienced by those taking the tricyclic antidepressants, are not a problem with SSRIs. Patients don't have to follow any sort of special diet, as they would with MAOIs, and the SSRIs don't produce the kinds of anticholinergic side effects the TCAs do. Patients generally find the side effects of the SSRIs less troublesome than those of either the TCAs or the MAOIs.

Other Newer Antidepressant and Antipanic Agents

Other of the newer agents are more complex in terms of their pharmacological actions. Some affect the neurotransmitters norepinephrine and dopamine, others work primarily on the norepinephrine and serotonin systems, and still others are a bit more complicated, but all of them share a tendency to affect one or some combination of the neurotransmitters just mentioned. Some will undoubtedly prove more useful than others in panic disorders and the related anxiety disorders. The Food and Drug Administration has for many years published guidelines regarding the disorders for which medications are felt to be most useful, but doctors have long treated patients with medications that were "off-label" according to those guidelines, because clinical judgment called for their use. Some of the newer medicines have not yet had time to go through the required FDA scrutiny for use in conditions other than the first one for which the pharmaceutical house released them. Others simply elect not to go through the rigorous process of getting another "on-label" indication. Often doctors have to rely on clinical judgment based on knowledge of the basic pharmacological actions of the medications to make an educated guess as to whether the drugs might help in similar conditions.

Venlafaxine (Effexor) is a fairly recent addition, and it differs slightly from the SSRIs in that it is an inhibitor of the reuptake of both serotonin and norepinephrine, instead of just serotonin. (Norepinephrine is disposed of through reabsorption into the transmitting nerve cell in a manner similar to what happens to serotonin.) Because its pharmacologic actions are so broad, physicians need to be careful that patients taking the drug do not start running elevated blood pressures. This type of medication is known as a serotonin and norepinephrine reuptake inhibitor, or SNRI.

Serotonin antagonist and reuptake inhibitors (SARIs) constitute another group of antidepressant medications that have appeared recently. These medicines are rather complex in their pharmacologic actions. They block the serotonin-2 receptors (5-HT2) postsynaptically, but they are also weak presynaptic inhibitors of serotonin reuptake (see chapter 6). The first of this class to get released in the United States was trazodone (Desyrel), and, more recently, nefazodone (Serzone) has become available. Nefazodone has even more complicated actions, in that it is also a weak presynaptic inhibitor for the reuptake of norepinephrine.

Another medication useful in a variety of conditions is bupropion (Wellbutrin or Zyban), which is a presynaptic reuptake inhibitor of both norepinephrine and dopamine (see chapter 6). Wellbutrin is the name used in psychiatric circles, and Zyban is the trade name used in treatment of smoking cessation. Apparently the craving for tobacco is tied in with the dopaminergic neurotransmitter system, and the effect this medication has on that system reduces the craving. Physicians have to use care in prescribing bupropion because of a slightly increased risk of seizures, but it generally has fewer side effects in the area of sexuality than the SSRIs, and is usually well tolerated.

Mirtazapine (Remeron) is another of the newer medications. Its actions are even more complex, blocking postsynaptic transmission at serotonin-2 and serotonin-3 neurotransmitter sites (5-HT2 and 5-HT3). Also, presynaptically it blocks inhibitory alpha-2-autoreceptors on noradrenergic neurons and alpha-2-heteroreceptors on serotonergic neurons. (Activating these receptors tends to block transmission of the nerve impulse, so blocking these inhibitory receptors helps to "turn on" the neurotransmission.) In addition to all this, the increased firing of the presynaptic noradrenergic neuron tends to increase the firing of serotonergic neurons (see chapter 6). So far, this drug has proved useful primarily in the depressive disorders. It is one of the agents that can cause agranulocytosis (a condition marked by a severe decrease in the number of certain types of white blood cells).

Benzodiazepines

Benzodiazepines used to be known as "minor tranquilizers." Under the wrong circumstances they tend to be habituating, but, when used correctly, they are very useful in the treatment of panic disorder and agoraphobia. These medications, such as alprazolam, lorazepam, clorazepate, and clonazepam, do not work directly on the neurotransmitters just discussed, but instead on one called GABA. It is one of the major neurotransmitters in the brain, and tends, in general, to be inhibitory in nature. Most of the benzodiazepines help with symptoms of generalized anxiety, but one in particular, alprazolam, helps to ward off actual panic attacks, not just anticipatory anxiety. Major differences among the benzodiazepines involve the speed at which they start working and the length of time they continue acting in the body. Some of them simply take a long time to be disposed of by the body, but others are more complicated, because they are converted to related chemicals that work in a similar pharmacological way.

Buspirone

Buspirone (Buspar), which is not a benzodiazepine and is nonhabituating, helps in treating anxiety disorders as well as depression. It has a very narrow pharmacological mode of action, and seems to have little to do with GABA. It is a serotonin-1A partial agonist, meaning that it maintains transmission on this receptor at some midpoint, instead of either antagonizing it or triggering it outright. Because of its specificity, this drug is useful in a variety of psychiatric conditions for fine-tuning other psychotropic medications when clinicians seek minor adjustments. One of its major advantages is its lack of habituation potential.

Mood Stabilizers

Certain medications that stabilize mood can also prove useful in the treatment of the anxiety disorders, including panic disorder. These include lithium, carbamazepine (Tegretol), valproic acid (Depakote), clonazepam (Klonopin), and gabapentin (Neurontin).

Lithium is a chemical element, compounds of which are used for disorders of mood instability (see chapter 2), and for mood stabilization in general, but its mechanism of action is still not clear, in spite of its being used now for many years. While most of the medications used in psychiatry work, in some fashion, through specific neurotransmitter systems, research done on lithium shows that it probably does not focus on any specific neurotransmitter system but instead works on a second-messenger system, probably triggered by its reaction with G-proteins in the membranes of nerve cells. In particular, its involvement with second-transmitter systems seems related to its inhibition of an enzyme involved in the phosphoinositide (PI) system. These second-messenger systems are quite pervasive, and would help to explain lithium's far-reaching effects. Also, the involvement of second messenger systems contributes to the difficulty researchers have had in pinning down any particular neurotransmitter system associated with lithium, since the medication affects so many of them. Researchers feel that these second messengers are, in turn, affecting intracellular metabolism in complex ways. Pharmaceutical houses usually supply lithium as the salt lithium carbonate (see chapter 6).

Carbamazepine (Tegretol) first found its niche as an anticonvulsant medication, but it soon proved helpful in disorders of mood instability as well. It seems to work on peripheral benzodiazepine receptors. Valproic acid (Depakote, Depakene) is another medication that originally was used as an anticonvulsant but which soon found its way into the psychiatric area. It seems to more directly enhance the effect of GABA. Clonazepam (Klonopin) is a high-potency, long-acting benzodiazepine, also originally used as an anticonvulsant and now beneficial in the area of mood instability. A newer agent, yet another anticonvulsant, gabapentin (Neurontin), is showing promise in the treatment of mood instability, but its mechanism of action is not yet clear. Other newer anticonvulsants being studied are lamotrigine (Lamictal), felbamate (Felbatol), topiramate (Topamax), and fosphenytoin (Cerebyx), but their usefulness in mood instability is not yet clearly established.

When lithium, carbamazepine, and valproic acid are being used, periodic attention should be paid to blood levels. Patients who take lithium may sometimes develop trouble with their thyroid function (often becoming hypothyroid) or with untoward effects on their kidneys, but monitoring of such potential problems is fairly easy through blood and urine tests. Those using carbamazepine and valproic acid should have their livers checked occasionally, as well as having blood counts done, to head off any potential trouble with adverse effects on liver function or decreasing blood counts.

Carbamazepine can cause agranulocytosis or aplastic anemia, both serious problems with the production, respectively, of certain white blood cells and of red blood cells. Patients taking valproic acid need to be watched primarily for liver problems and for thrombocytopenia (a disorder involving platelet counts so low that the blood doesn't clot as quickly as it should).

Antipsychotics

Antipsychotic medications have been around for some time. Depending on the patient's symptoms, these drugs may prove useful in treating panic disorder, although they are not the first medicines doctors think of for this condition.

One of the mainstays in the treatment of schizophrenia, antipsychotics include chlorpromazine (Thorazine), thioridazine (Mellaril), loxapine (Loxitane), molindone (Moban), haloperidol (Haldol), thiothixene (Navane), trifluoperazine (Stelazine), fluphenazine (Prolixin), and perphenazine (Trilafon). Among the newer "atypical" antipsychotics are clozapine (Clozaril), risperidone (Risperidal), olanzepine (Zyprexa), and quetiapine (Seroquel). These medications are called atypical because they are less likely to cause the movement disturbances that are characteristic of the older agents and because of subtle changes in their antagonism to dopamine transmission, as well as to that of some other neurotransmitters, such as serotonin.

The first antipsychotic was chlorpromazine (Thorazine), and other typical antipsychotic medications (neuroleptics) soon followed. These medications worked quite well to help control the so-called "positive symptoms" of schizophrenia, i.e., hallucinations, delusions, and bizarre behavior, but a problem with the drugs was that they didn't do much to alleviate the "negative symptoms," namely poverty of facial expression (flat or inappropriate affect), difficulty putting one thought behind another (thought blocking and looseness of associations), apathy, and a general inability to enjoy life (anhedonia). The classical antipsychotic agents mostly worked by blocking the action of dopamine at the dopamine-2 (D2) receptor, but the newer, atypical antipsychotics have a more complicated pharmacological profile, some of them also blocking serotonin receptors. For example, clozapine (Clozaril) blocks quite a few neurotransmitter systems, including dopamine-1, -2, and -4 (D1, D2, D4) and serotonin-1C, -2C, and -3 (5-HT1C, 5-HT2C, and 5-HT3). Also, it is quite anticholinergic. Clozapine's most notorious side effect is that it causes decreased white blood cell count or even the very serious agranulocytosis, in which the bone marrow's white blood cell production virtually shuts down. This possibility caused the Food and Drug Administration to require very costly and frequent monitoring of a patient's blood levels in order to permit the medication's distribution. Most of the other newer antipsychotic medications have not had such potentially dangerous side effects. Risperidone, another newer antipsychotic, blocks D2 but also 5-HT2A and 5-HT2C. Various other newer antipsychotic agents block different combinations of receptors, but they all seem to block dopamine and serotonin transmission to one degree or another. These newer agents appear to have less of a tendency to cause a potentially permanent movement disorder called tardive dyskinesia than the older antipsychotic medications did.

Another problem occasionally caused primarily by the older antipsychotic medicines is neuroleptic malignant syndrome. In this disorder, the patient's muscles become very stiff, and there is a clouding of the person's consciousness with a high fever. This is a very serious condition that can result in death. The doctor has to take the patient off the drug and sometimes give medications to reverse the antipsychotic's antagonism to dopamine. A common dilemma is that neuroleptic malignant syndrome can resemble catatonia, for which antipsychotics are one of the treatments.

Medications for Attention-Deficit Hyperactivity Disorder (ADHD)

For attention-deficit hyperactivity disorder (see chapter 2), behavior modification and alterations in study and work environments are frequently helpful, but pharmacological measures may be needed. Medications include dextroamphetamine (Dexedrine), combinations of dextroamphetamine and amphetamine (Adderall), methamphetamine (Desoxyn), methylphenidate (Ritalin), and pemoline (Cylert). Although these drugs sometimes have a place in the treatment of panic disorder, their use is problematic, since they can cause panic to get worse. Sometimes ADHD calls for other agents, such as imipramine, desipramine, venlafaxine, or bupropion, and in severe cases antipsychotics or lithium may be necessary.

People often ask how long they will have to be on medication for panic disorder, but the answer to this question is not simple. Doctors have to make sure that patients are able to tolerate the medicine, and the dosage has to be adjusted to take care of the target symptoms. If the medication isn't at the right dose, it's not going to help much; in fact, sometimes the patient gets only the side effects without deriving any therapeutic benefit. Then the doctor has to make sure the medication is continuing to do what it's supposed to do. Another problem is that some people have an emotional aversion to taking any sort of medicine, especially one they feel has been stigmatized as a psychiatric drug. Those who might be willing to take penicillin if they had pneumonia or who ingest caffeine every morning may feel great embarrassment at the notion of taking fluoxetine to help themselves function better emotionally.

Those being treated for panic disorder are frequently placed on a smaller starting dosage of antidepressant medication than that used for depression, with it often being increased to a higher maintenance dosage. It is common for individuals with panic disorder to be more sensitive to minor side effects that make them "feel funny" than are people with depression, since those "funny" feelings are often similar to the ones that herald the onset of a panic attack. Another complication is that sometimes when the medication is started the panic attacks actually get slightly worse for a brief period of time.

Sometimes, for reasons that are poorly understood, medicines just stop working. New medications are continually reaching the market and sometimes patients and doctors simply want to try a different one to see if it works better and has fewer side reactions. At some point in the course of treatment, after the symptoms are under control, the patient and the doctor begin to reassess the ongoing need for the medicine, and at what dose. Naturally, cutting back on the dosage or discontinuing the medicine altogether involves the risk that the original symptoms will return. This consideration has to be weighed carefully against the side effects of the medicine, the inconvenience of taking it, and the cost. (Some are quite expensive.) Patients with panic disorder are often more accepting of long-term treatment with medications than are some other kinds of patients, because they dread so intensely the prospect of the panic attacks returning. Sometimes it's quite clear that social stressors and phase-of-life problems contributed heavily to the onset of the panic disorder, so that the patient and doctor eventually feel it's worth taking a chance by cutting back on the medication and seeing whether symptoms recur or whether the syndrome seems to have disappeared. The discontinuation of medication has to be approached cautiously, however. Since there is such a strong biological component in susceptibility to panic disorder, sufferers are often wise to stay on medication to minimize the possibility of recurrence.

Clinical Case #1   A twenty-one-year-old woman who had never had any psychiatric problems before was feeling a certain amount of pressure in college, and was having some minor disagreements with her boyfriend; in general, there was more stress on her than usual. One night, while she was sitting in the library at school studying for a test, her heart suddenly started racing uncontrollably. She became short of breath, and felt as though she were "going crazy." She asked someone to drive her to the emergency room, where she had an EKG and was examined by the doctor there, but no general medical explanation for the problem was found. She went on about her business as usual, although with some trepidation, since she was concerned that another episode might occur.

About two weeks later, a second panic attack occurred when the young woman was driving to her boyfriend's house, and she had to pull over to the side of the road. After about an hour, the symptoms gradually subsided. She went to her local doctor the next day, and he placed her on a low dosage of alprazolam (0.25 mg twice a day) for the anxiety. She noticed only minimal effect from the medicine at this dose. She was unable to go on attending school or to keep up with social obligations. The general medical tests continued to be uninformative, so her family doctor referred her to a psychiatrist. The family history showed that her mother had always been "nervous," and the patient said that her aunt had had a "nervous breakdown," with a lot of anxiety, which could have been panic disorder.

The young woman was found to have panic disorder, and the psychiatrist placed her on paroxetine at a dosage of 20 mg each morning, with the dosage of alprazolam being increased to 1.0 mg three times a day. She called the doctor back in two days to say that she was too drowsy during the daytime, which appeared to be related to the timing of the paroxetine dose, so the psychiatrist told her to take that at bedtime. Three days later she returned to the clinic for follow-up. She was generally less anxious, with panic attacks now happening only about once a week and seeming to be less intense and of shorter duration. The doctor told her to start keeping a record of situations that were anxiety-provoking for her, such as driving, going into stores, or going back to the library where the first episode had happened, so that they could study the journal during sessions. She continued to see the psychiatrist every week or two. Eventually the full-blown panic attacks stopped completely, but the patient reported that she still felt "trapped" in certain situations. Patient and doctor continued to discuss the best way to approach anxiety-provoking situations, so that she could deal with them in a gradual way that would cause only moderate, manageable anxiety. The young woman continued taking the medication, and she was able to get back to her studies in about four weeks.

By approximately four months later, the patient felt that she was about 90 percent back to where she had previously been emotionally, but she still harbored a dread that the panic attacks would return. She began to need fewer and fewer sessions with the psychiatrist, and by the end of five years she did not require any medications. She looked back on the whole ordeal with a certain embarrassment, wondering, "What the heck was going on with me back then?"

Psychotherapeutic Approaches

Despite the many advances in the availability of medications for the anxiety disorders, psychotherapy in its various forms continues to be a mainstay in the treatment of these conditions. We will examine the following kinds of psychotherapeutic approaches: (1) cognitive restructuring and relaxation training, (2) family therapy and family factors, and (3) psychodynamic approaches.

Cognitive Restructuring and Relaxation Training

Cognitive-behavioral therapy was developed in the 1960s by Dr. Aaron Beck. In this approach, patient and therapist

search for thoughts and feelings that contribute to the anxi-
eties leading to panic attacks. Persons with anxiety disorders
such as panic disorder frequently suffer from distortions in
thinking that unnecessarily promote anxiety and feelings
of depression. Steering the patient away from such counterproductive tendencies diminishes the level of anxiety or
depression. People frequently develop habits in their thinking
that involve overgeneralizations, jumping to conclusions, and
magnifying the negative aspects of things. They may find
themselves waging war against problems needlessly or against
problems that don't even exist (of course, problems that
don't exist are impossible to solve). Correcting such habits of
thinking can help patients adjust better to life's unavoidable
stresses. Cognitive therapy focuses to a greater degree on the
here-and-now than do some other forms of therapy that are
more concerned with circumstances in the past.

The use of behavioral techniques can sometimes stop
the onset of a panic attack. The patient often gets into a
cycle of sensing the first symptoms of a panic attack and
then fueling the problem by adding another layer of anxiety,
bringing about a full-blown attack. It is quite helpful if this
self-defeating cycle can be interrupted. Since hyperventilation
contributes to the escalation of anxiety, it is important for a
person to practice breathing correctly during times of stress.
Other anxiety-reducing strategies can be explored with the
therapist. Patients are often unaware of the level of stress
in their lives and can benefit from training in relaxation
techniques. Progressive muscular relaxation exercises and
even biofeedback can be helpful. In biofeedback therapy
patients are connected to a machine that monitors their unconscious bodily functions, such as heart rate, breathing rate,
and galvanic skin response (the electrical resistance between
two points on the surface of the skin). The readout on these
levels is then displayed or made audible so that the patient
can be trained to steer away from the thoughts and feelings
that are promoting further anxiety. Persons suffering from

agoraphobia sometimes require a structured program for facing "dangerous" situations in a gradually increasing way, so that they can fight the avoidant tendencies that are restricting their activities. This step-by-step approach allows them to master their fears a bit at a time, without the triggering of a panic attack.

One of the key elements in the development of panic attacks is the patient's hypersensitivity to proprioceptive sensations, i.e., internal sensations often having to do with movement and position of the body. Most people don't pay much attention to these, but to patients with panic disorder such sensations (including dizziness, lightheadedness, and minor gastrointestinal symptoms) frequently herald the onset of a panic attack. Patients who are worried about recurring panic attacks tend to become sensitive to these internal proprioceptive messages, and this can start a chain reaction of gradually increasing anxiety. If persons are exposed to these sensations in small doses, they can become desensitized and get used to the idea that this situation does not always indicate the onset of another panic attack. Often a particular situation will be associated with one of these sensations, so that therapists can take advantage of the opportunity to gradually expose patients to the stimuli in a controlled fashion, with the result that less anxiety will occur in the future. For example, if going to a certain store has caused the patient problems in the past, it is often helpful to have him or her just drive past the store at first and deal with the sensations that are bothersome at that low level of exposure. Then the person can sit in the parking lot outside the store and work on controlling the sensations in that somewhat more anxiety-provoking situation. Finally the individual can reach the point of going into the store and can start desensitizing himself or herself to that experience. It helps for patients to get used to these sorts of situations over a period of perhaps twenty or thirty minutes, instead of simply approaching whatever it is and then immediately backing away. If patients stay in the problem situation for a reasonable period of time without feeling overwhelming anxiety, they will be able to see that a panic attack doesn't occur. If, however, they only approach the dreaded situation for a few moments and then retreat, the anxiety doesn't have a chance to dissipate and may even be reinforced.

Researchers are finding that there are at least two different anxiety programs in the brain. One has to do with the so-called higher thinking areas, and the other involves responses to more subtle, subliminal cues to which the mind becomes sensitized.

Some of the stressors that people face in life are directly related to their temperaments and personalities, which may give them a higher natural setting for anxiety than others have. The contribution of the temperament factor is often forgotten when the clinician is considering the development of the anxiety disorders, but it is one of the major emotional variables, and it seems to be inherited. Some people, from childhood on, are especially shy, cautious, and inhibited. They are often a bit more fearful than others, and seem to be more "on edge." They handle new situations with a higher degree of stress, and generally need more reassurance. These people frequently have difficulty with a greater-than-usual sense of attachment and loss, although this can sometimes be attributed to their having been overprotected or under-protected as children, and may have little to do with innate, biological temperament. Such individuals often have many worries about their health or about potential disasters, since, after all, death is the ultimate generator of the anxiety of separation. Some also have an exaggerated need to exercise control in their lives. While most people realize that there are limitations on what they can manage in their environments, in some this lack of absolute control stirs up a great deal of anxiety, moving them closer to panic attacks. Anxiety can also be generated by a lack of self-confidence, which may come from several different sources and be a persistent thorn in the patient's side. Some people are plagued by personality traits that make them try to avoid having emotions, especially negative ones, which makes it hard to be logical about the impact of feelings on their lives.

Behaviorists have observed that some persons seem driven to an unhealthy degree by an inordinate emphasis on deadlines and "beating the clock." Those who belong to this so-called "type A personality" group also tend to be perfectionistic and to suffer from chronic frustration. People with this type of personality set themselves up for gradually increasing stress and its accompanying anxiety. (The condition has even been linked to premature atherosclerotic heart disease, as well as to other medical disturbances.) In contrast, those with "type B personality" are less bothered by self-imposed deadline pressure, perfectionism, and frustrations. Cognitive-behavioral therapy can be helpful in gradually changing the more anxiety-inducing "type A" patterns into the more relaxed "type B" style.

Another helpful suggestion is for patients to carry a list of reassurances or instructions with them that will be easily available when a panic attack starts. This may include a reminder that the panic attack is a psychiatric symptom that will be limited in time, reassurance that the person is not dying or "going crazy," instructions for avoiding hyperventilation, or notations about what has helped previously in similar situations. (Patients facing a panic attack often have difficulty concentrating so that they can't remember advice or techniques that have proved helpful before.)

Patients can get great relief from panic attack symptoms if they can learn to breathe correctly and to refrain from hyperventilating. Although breathing is usually an unconscious activity, it can be brought under conscious control. Breathing patterns can have a strong effect on a person's level of anxiety and also on his or her general sense of well-being. As we have seen, some people start to hyperventilate at the slightest provocation, which tends to generate more anxiety. The typical automatic response in anxious persons is that of rapid, shallow breathing, which makes the person's blood more alkaline by driving off carbon dioxide, and, in a vicious cycle, makes the anxiety escalate. Some people tend chronically to hyperventilate, which can cause changes in their blood chemistry, making them even more prone to anxiety by limiting the ability of the blood to "buffer" pH changes coming from an anxiety attack. Practicing to reduce this chronic tendency to hyperventilate can help correct the chronic blood chemistry changes that make it easier for panic attacks to start, and also helps make people aware of the significant effect that correct breathing can have on their sense of emotional well-being. It's important for a person with a tendency to hyperventilate to learn how to breathe deeply and slowly. Practice is essential, because when people are very anxious they don't have the time to think about correct breathing or the concentration to bring to bear. If they haven't been practicing to the point that proper breathing has become second nature, they have trouble putting it into effect.

Another helpful exercise is to keep a journal that includes details about what the circumstances were at the time of a panic attack, the sensations involved, and which thoughts or behaviors seemed to help or to make the situation worse. Patient and therapist can use this record to put together a strategy for coping with these episodes. This also helps patients to concentrate on what's actually going on, instead of automatically magnifying the sense of danger.

Patients should understand that they have something akin to homework to do in between their meetings with the doctor. A slightly different kind of journal keeping involves making a record of what kinds of things provoke sensations of panic and what alleviates those feelings. Structured hierarchies of anxiety-provoking situations can be arranged so that patients can gradually learn to face them and to desensitize themselves without overdoing it all at once. People learn from their successes and failures. Individuals who have frequent panic attacks start to overreact to the first sensations of one. In contrast, those who use cognitive-behavioral techniques are managing the situation better, less allowing the panic attacks to get the best of them.

Family Therapy and Family Factors

Families often get involved directly or indirectly, voluntarily or inadvertently, in helping patients overcome their problems with panic disorder. They usually need to be advised on how to be encouraging to the patient without seeming oblivious to the problem and how to be helpful without shouldering undue responsibility in a counterproductive way. Sometimes well-meaning relatives get into the trap of "enabling" by continually providing a family member who has anxiety with a means for avoiding problem situations. Being overly sympathetic can have unexpected, counterproductive effects, such as reinforcing maladaptive habits and dependent behavior. A patient's family needs to understand that the person has to learn to be able to face difficult situations so as not to stay dependent on those with good intentions who are always available, for example, to run errands. Another danger is that families sometimes unconsciously promote certain roles for their members, so that there may be an unrecognized resistance to someone breaking out of the role of sick person.

Clinical Case #2   This thirty-five-year-old housewife with two children had functioned reasonably well for most of her life, although she had always been slightly "on edge." She began gradually to have periods in which she felt lightheaded, but she passed them off, attributing them to having drunk too much coffee. She cut back on the caffeine consumption, but the periods persisted and became more frequent. While attending one of her son's soccer games, she suddenly had the first full-blown panic attack, with chest pain, shortness of breath, and an uncomfortable feeling that things "weren't

real." Feeling as though her head were spinning, she was
convinced that she was "going crazy" or dying or both. The
woman was taken to her general practitioner, who placed
her in the hospital for twenty-four hours and had tests done
to make sure she wasn't suffering from some sort of heart
condition or stroke, but the tests revealed little except a fast
heart rate. The general practitioner thought that it was an
anxiety attack, but both he and the patient were puzzled as to
why it would have happened then. The woman was placed on
5 mg of diazepam twice per day as needed, but she began to
be afraid of going to public places, worrying about potential
embarrassment. Her panic attacks increased in frequency,
to the point that they were occurring about every other day.
She ended up having to go to the emergency room several
times, where the personnel did a number of general medical
tests, but none of them showed anything significant except for
occasional slightly elevated blood pressure, noted at the time
of the anxiety.

One of the emergency room doctors finally sent her to a
psychiatrist, saying, with some hesitancy, that he thought she
might have panic disorder. She was placed on fluoxetine at
20 mg each morning, and the diazepam was replaced with
lorazepam at 1.0 mg three times per day, partly because the
patient was dissatisfied with the diazepam since it hadn't
helped much yet. Gradually, the panic attacks decreased to
about one every two weeks, but by this time the patient had
become afraid to leave the house; in fact, she was reluctant
even to leave her bedroom. Her husband was missing work
to help take care of the children, and she felt guilty about
the entire situation, which made the emotional problem
even worse. The psychiatrist referred her to a psychologist
who could help her work out a specific plan for gradually
pushing herself to do more so as to overcome the agoraphobia problem, now that the panic attacks were under better
control. The patient continued to feel guilty and embarrassed
about the entire situation. Her family and friends couldn't

understand what was wrong with her, in spite of her attempts to explain to them that it was panic disorder. After three or four months had passed, she was able to return to most of her customary activities, but she was still afraid that the panic attacks would recur. Several years later she decided that she wanted to try doing without the fluoxetine, so she and her psychiatrist agreed that she would stop, and the panic attacks didn't return. She continued to keep lorazepam on hand, however, "as a safety net, just in case," and she reduced her visits to the psychiatrist to once every three months.

Psychodynamic Approaches

Although less used in recent times, psychodynamic psychotherapy and psychoanalysis itself (several schools of it) continue to survive in a fashion complementary to the biological and the more behavioral approaches to treatment. (The decrease in use of psychotherapy has to do partly with economic considerations, since, on the surface, this type of treatment seems more time consuming and therefore more costly than the biological and behavioral approaches.)

The basis of psychodynamics is the observation that patients automatically take on a variety of defense mechanisms to avoid distress and to control impulses that are unacceptable to society (see chapter 3). These mechanisms are unconscious (although sometimes specific behaviors associated with them aren't), and the less adaptive ones often contribute to the patient's unhappiness, but getting the person to recognize the habits of thinking and acting that are contributing to his or her problems can be difficult. Such habits often result in the anxiety and depression that lead to panic disorder, and the psychotherapist must show the patient in a meaningful way how this is the case. Constructive changes in these areas can often be made to the patient's emotional benefit. Sometimes a person feels or acts regarding present situations in a way that resembles past behavior in similar circumstances. In fact, the patient often displaces these feelings and thoughts onto the therapists themselves (transference), which may either serve as a useful illustration of the habit or prove disruptive to therapy. For example, some people tend to place blame elsewhere for all of their problems, while others internalize conflicts so that they feel anxious and depressed or even develop physical illnesses. Much of the work of psychotherapy addresses these defense mechanisms; gradual adjustments to them are made, so that stress has less of an impact. This approach toward psychotherapy requires a certain amount of finesse, because sometimes uncovering thoughts and feelings from the past can temporarily cause an increase in the patient's overall level of anxiety and depression. If the patient's symptoms are severe, it is often best to postpone psychodynamic work until the situation is somewhat under control.

Because psychodynamic psychotherapy can be more time consuming and therefore less cost effective than patients and physicians consider desirable, what is called "brief psychotherapy" has recently been developed. This approach involves an attempt on the part of therapist and patient to be focused from the outset, so that, even though the therapy remains psychodynamic in nature, the work is done in a more efficient way. Sometimes a specified number of sessions or time period is designated in which to accomplish the treatment. Again, a good deal of skill is required on the part of the therapist, since this form of treatment can be temporarily anxiety-provoking.

Psychotherapy in general is a rather tricky field and involves at least as much art as it does science. A psychiatrist with experience and good clinical judgment will be able to time observations correctly and to keep patients from getting so frustrated that they stop listening. One of the challenges of treating people with unconscious, maladaptive habits involves what is known as "resistance." One might assume that patients would want to get rid of whatever habit is making them miserable, but it's often not so. They may be afraid of facing the problem and actually feel secure with the misery they are used to. Patients in this condition often start missing or arriving late for therapy sessions, intellectualizing, finding excuses, taking frustrations out on friends and family—in other words, doing everything except making straightforward progress.

Often the most useful and realistic approach to treatment for a patient who has panic disorder is combination therapy, involving medication and some form of psychotherapy, usually cognitive-behavioral therapy.

Clinical Case #3   This forty-five-year-old man worked as a stockbroker. He had always tended to be outgoing and gregarious, and often jokingly referred to his "type A" personality. After a particularly hectic week, he went to a large shopping mall, and, while walking around in a bookstore, suddenly began to feel lightheaded and to notice a queasy sensation. He went to a corner bench outside in the mall area to rest, but the panicky sensations, now including a racing heartbeat and shortness of breath, got worse, until finally abating after about thirty minutes. He called his family doctor, who told him to come in for an exam. After several tests to rule out the more common types of general medical conditions, the doctor said he thought the man had had an anxiety attack. The doctor placed him on clorazepate, which lessened the man's general level of apprehension, but two days later another panic attack happened at work. His doctor urged him to see a psychiatrist, and, finally, with great hesitancy, he did. The psychiatrist asked him many questions about his past and upbringing, and changed his medication to sertraline 50 mg each day and clonazepam 1.0 mg twice a day. In addition, they talked about the patient's inordinate need to achieve, which seemed to some degree to stem from feelings of inferiority during his childhood. The psychiatrist warned him that all the medicine in the world wouldn't help unless he learned to slow down a bit.

Over the next few weeks the panic attacks persisted, but gradually became less frequent and less intense. The man discovered that taking the medicine was the easy part; changing his "type A" habits proved more challenging. His habitual focus on deadlines and "beating the clock" were deeply ingrained personality traits that the patient found himself pursuing in an automatic, unconscious way that was hard to stop. The psychiatrist helped him find ways to modify this behavior, such as driving below a certain speed to and from work or leaving his wristwatch locked in a desk drawer for part of the day. Often, however, this approach turned out to be ineffective with him, and the best course was for him to leave the house earlier for any sort of appointment or deadline. Eventually, the panic attacks stopped entirely, but the patient's background level of anxiety persisted. He stayed on the sertraline, with the clonazepam used only on an "as needed" basis. Eventually, however, he learned to pay closer attention to his limitations and to pace himself better, so that his general level of anxiety gradually diminished. He found, though, that he needed reminders to put the brakes on his "deadline crisis mentality," and would leave himself notes to that effect or even on occasion force himself deliberately to be late for appointments. He also finally started taking everyone's perennial advice that he actually take time off for vacations. After about three years, his level of general anxiety decreased, and he and the psychiatrist began to talk about cutting the sertraline dosage in half, proceeding with caution, to see what would happen.

Alternative Approaches

Several herbs have gained notoriety for their putative ability to help with symptoms of anxiety and depression, but, since research on them is not generally as thorough as for standard FDA-approved medications, their usefulness and safety are hard to assess. Many people believe in the help afforded by St. John's wort (*Hypericum*), kava kava (*Piper methysticum*), gingko biloba, the B vitamins (especially folic acid, vitamin B-6, and vitamin B-12), and omega-3 fatty acids (such as EPA and DHA), but their efficacy is not clear. (Apparently, researchers have studied St. John's wort much more thoroughly in Germany, where it is said to be prescribed more often than Prozac.) One of the problems in such situations is that sufferers may resort to these less orthodox approaches instead of getting the help they need from the generally safer and more efficacious standard psychiatric treatments.

6. Searching for Answers

We will now look at some recent research.

Medication Levels and Interactions

As we have seen, the question of medication dosage is frequently a complex one. Physicians tend to have mixed feelings about getting levels on various medications and about how the interpret the medication levels after they are drawn. Only a few antidepressants have clearly recognized therapeutic serum drug levels (these include amitriptyline, bupropion, clomipramine, desipramine, doxepin, imipramine, nortriptyline, and protriptyline), and much is unavoidably left to a doctor's clinical judgment. It's easy to oversimplify treatment decisions, basing them solely on blood levels, but to do so often causes problems. Much of the difficulty arises because of the distant relationship between blood levels of a medication and the concentration of the drug in the brain at the actual synapses, but the level at the synapses isn't the whole story either. (Many chemicals cannot find their way into the brain from the bloodstream at all, because of the blood-brain barrier, which prevents their penetration.)

Another complex area involves drug interactions, of which there are three primary types: pharmacodynamic, pharmacokinetic, and pharmaceutical.

Pharmacodynamic interactions occur when the action of one drug is changed by the action of another one without any change in the first drug's concentration. These are generally more difficult to quantify and interpret than pharmacokinetic interactions, in which one drug actually influences the concentration of another. An example of a pharmacodynamic interaction is the additive tendency toward sedation that happens when the old-fashioned antihistamines are mixed with either benzodiazepines or alcohol; another is the tendency for monoamine oxidase inhibitors to interact with some medications and with foods to elevate blood pressure.

Pharmacokinetic interactions can occur at several different sites. One involves absorption from the gastrointestinal tract. For example, certain medications that change the pH (amount of acidity or alkalinity) of the GI tract can interfere with the absorption of other medicines that must cross this barrier at a certain pH. Also, some medications can influence the activity of enzymes in the gut wall so that other medicines are handled differently, some being metabolized before they can even penetrate into the bloodstream. After they are in the bloodstream, other potential interactions include the tendency for one medication to displace another when they must compete for chemical binding with serum proteins, such as albumin. Many of the antidepressants travel in the bloodstream by being bound to these proteins, and if two medications are vying for available positions on the proteins it can alter the amount of the drug that is freely available in unbound form. (The medication that's bound to the serum protein does not usually leave the bloodstream, since the protein itself doesn't; it's the unbound part that's available to diffuse into the tissues.) Eventually, most medications pass through the hepatic portal vein and are filtered through the liver, where much of their metabolism occurs. The gauntlet of metabolic degradation processes that drugs taken by mouth have to go through before reaching the general systemic circulation is known as "first pass phenomenon."

One area of research receiving a lot of attention recently involves the cytochrome P450 system, a collection of enzymes involved in the breakdown of many medications of varying types. It is located in the liver, as well as in the gut wall and in several other tissues. Sometimes one medicine will alter the concentration of another because it is competing for the same enzyme system. Since the second medication can't get to the enzyme, it isn't broken down as fast, and, consequently, its concentration tends to increase. Some medications are not just jockeying competitively for sites for metabolic break-down, but are, in fact, directly increasing or decreasing the speed of the enzyme in metabolizing the other medicine. (Researchers call the direct increase in enzymatic activity "induction," and the decrease is "inhibition.") Reading the package inserts for various medications can be quite confusing even for professionals, but especially for patients unfamiliar with the medical terminology. Many of the enumerated details are given because of governmental regulations and the need for legal disclaimers. The Food and Drug Administration has gradually been increasing the general level of scrutiny and the requirements for package insert information before authorizing the release of medications to the public. Consequently, it appears at times that some of the newer medicines are more dangerous than the older agents, when, in fact, they may have been subjected to more rigorous testing and reporting requirements.

Some examples of cytochrome P450 activity are as follows:

Cytochrome P450 1A2 System: Several unlikely-sounding factors such as smoking cigarettes and eating charcoal-broiled foods or cruciferous vegetables increase (induce) the activity of this enzyme system, but the antidepressant fluvoxamine tends to inhibit it. This enzyme system breaks down certain pharmaceutically active substances, including caffeine, theophylline, and aminophylline (the latter two used in treating asthma), as well as psychotropic medications such as imipramine, amitriptyline, and clomipramine. If patients on one of these medicines have their conditions stabilized and then suddenly start smoking, for example, doctors may find that they have to increase the dosage. This is because the patients are metabolizing the substrates (the chemicals broken down by the enzyme) faster, clearing them more quickly from their systems. In contrast, doctors placing patients on fluvoxamine may find that the patients require a lesser dosage of the substrate medications. Since fluvoxamine inhibits the enzymatic processes, more of these substrates should be left around unmetabolized, the liver breaking them down more slowly.

Cytochrome P450 2C9/19 System: This enzyme system is inhibited by fluoxetine, sertraline, and fluvoxamine, and is important in the metabolic breakdown of imipramine, amitriptyline, clomipramine, and diazepam, as well as of the anticonvulsant medicine phenytoin, the anticoagulant warfarin, and the antidiabetic medication tolbutamide. This means that patients placed on one of these inhibitory antidepressants can end up with higher blood levels of any of these latter substrates. It should be noted that the 2C19 subfamily is deficient in 18 percent of Japanese-Americans and African-Americans but only 4 percent of Caucasians, and there is a higher probability of difficulties with poor metabolism by this enzyme system in populations more likely to have the deficiency.

Cytochrome P450 2D6 System: Fluoxetine, sertraline, and paroxetine tend to inhibit the activity of this enzyme system, which is involved in the metabolism of the SSRIs, the TCAs, neuroleptic medications, and certain antihypertensive medications, such as propranolol and metoprolol. Among Caucasians, 7 to 10 percent have a genetic problem with this enzyme system, whereas only 1 to 4 percent of African-Americans do; Asians don't appear to have the problem.

Cytochrome P450 2E System: Alcohol (ethanol) and INH, an antitubercular drug, appear to induce this enzyme system so that it works more rapidly, in contrast to its inhibition by TCAs, some antipsychotic medications, and flurazepam.

Cytochrome P450 3A4 System: This enzyme system contributes about 30 percent of the cytochrome P450 present in the liver and about 70 percent of that in the gut wall. It seems gradually to decline in activity as a person ages, which means that younger people typically require higher doses of metabolized medications than older persons. The strongest inhibitors of this enzyme system are certain antifungal drugs, such as ketoconazole (Nizoral), and the macrolide antibiotics, such as erythromycin and clarithromycin (Biaxin). Fluoxetine, sertraline, and fluvoxamine, as well as another antidepressant, nefazadone (Serzone), also tend to inhibit it. It metabolizes several different medicines, and one has to be careful about mixing these agents together, because the inhibition of this enzyme system can cause a dangerous buildup of some of the newer medications, such as astemizole (Hismanal) and terfenidine (Seldane). The unexpected accumulation of these medications caused by enzyme inhibition can cause heart rhythm irregularities, some of which can be fatal. Carba-mazepine (Tegretol—a mood stabilizer and anticonvulsant), phenobarbital (another anticonvulsant), and dexamethazone (an anti-inflammatory steroid), can induce this enzyme system, resulting in a decrease in the concentrations of the corre-sponding substrates.

Imaging Studies and EEG

Several recent developments have allowed researchers in a variety of experimental settings to get a better idea of what the living brain looks like anatomically, as well as how it functions metabolically, in healthy individuals and in those with psychiatric disorders. These studies include the use of computerized axial tomography (CAT or CT scans), magnetic resonance imaging (MRI scans), positron emission tomog-raphy (PET scans), and single photon emission computed tomography (SPECT scans), as well as the older electroen-cephalogram (EEG). Results of these studies are preliminary, and have not yet shed enough light on the psychiatric disor-ders to have much impact on treatment.

Brain imaging techniques fall generally into two categories: those showing primarily structural abnormalities (CAT and MRI scans) and those showing function of the brain (PET and SPECT scans).

PET scans and SPECT scans indicate that patients having more blood flow near the right hippocampus versus the left hippocampus, in the temporal lobes, and a relative increase in the lower parts of the prefrontal areas appear to be more apt to develop panic attacks by lactate infusion than other individuals. Generalized anxiety itself seems accompanied by a reduction in blood flow to the frontal lobes. Also, MRI studies show that patients with panic disorder have more of a tendency to have structural abnormalities in the temporal lobes than do other subjects. In general, mild anxiety causes an increase in cerebral blood flow and metabolism, but, if the anxiety becomes severe, the blood flow tends to decrease. Hyperventilation caused by anxiety often reduces blood flow to the brain, and relatively low penetration of oxygen into the brain may relate to symptoms of severe anxiety. Infusions of epinephrine can cause significant anxiety in generalized anxiety disorder patients, but, curiously enough, it doesn't seem significantly to affect blood flow to the brain. (Perhaps this is because, at different sites, epinephrine sometimes dilates and at other times constricts smooth muscle, as found in blood vessel walls.)

A number of brain imaging studies involving the use of benzodiazepines have produced interesting findings. One study showed that long-term benzodiazepine use correlated with slight loss of brain tissue. One of the PET scan studies in patients with generalized anxiety disorder treated with benzodiazepines showed a reduction in metabolism in the visual areas of the brain and an increase in the metabolism in the thalamus and basal ganglia. Also, patients with generalized anxiety disorder treated with benzodiazepines showed a decrease in blood sugar metabolism in certain areas on the right side of the brain. These findings are not yet completely understood.

Schizophrenia has been the subject of many brain imaging studies, and these show a tendency toward enlargement of the lateral ventricles of the brain and away from the usual bilateral anatomical symmetry, with a general decrease in the volume of the gyri on the surface of the brain, as well as atrophy of the cerebellum and alterations in tissue density.

The electroencephalogram, which has been around for a long time, is a good test in some ways but rather limited in others. Its strong points are that it is not invasive and that it can be very sensitive in a variety of brain disorders, but its results are not very specific. Certain patterns, such as alpha waves, especially in the occipital areas, can show relaxation. A number of different conditions can result in the slowing of brain waves, which also change significantly with aging. Neurologists have to consider many different factors when interpreting EEGs, such as whether the patients are asleep or awake, what medications they may be on, how they are breathing, how old they are, and even whether their eyes are open or closed.

Substance P and Other Areas of Research

Discovered in 1931, substance P has emerged again recently as an area of interest for pharmaceutical researchers, who have been looking for such antagonists for many years and are beginning to find them. Substance P is a neuropeptide (similar to a protein but a bit shorter), and antagonists to it seem to act in an untraditional manner, i.e., without direct involvement in serotonin, norepinephrine, or dopamine circuits. Substance P is one of a number of peptides that are currently the subjects of research as to neurological activity; these include the endorphins, the enkephalins, and neuropeptide Y. Because the delay in reaction time of its antagonist is two to three weeks, similar to that of the more traditional antidepressants, researchers suspect that there is some final common pathway—a shared mechanism of action between the two groups of medications. This new form of antidepressant seems to have fewer side effects generally, but as of this writing (early 2000) the medication is not yet on the market in the United States. One of the main objects of research attention is an experimental substance P antagonist, MK-869. Psychiatrists are hoping that MK-869 or one of its cousins will soon be available. Researchers are finding substance P in areas such as the amygdala and hypothalamus, and its activity seems closely aligned with limbic function. Its antagonists appear to have both antianxiety and antidepressant actions and so offer hope for use in a wide variety of psychiatric disorders, including panic disorder. Researchers are also finding that increases in substance P activation correlate with the amount of stress a person experiences, which makes it a bit novel. With any luck we should be seeing the release of one or two of these substance P antagonists (SPAs)within the next few years.

Research is beginning to show more clearly that problems with specific limbic-related areas of the brain contribute to certain conditions, such as the association of the amygdala with panic attacks, of the hippocampus with posttraumatic stress disorder, and of the prefrontal cortex with generalized anxiety. In addition to research involving substance P, studies are under way with many other neuropeptides and related chemicals in and about the limbic system and the hypothalamo-pituitary axis, including blockers of corticotropin-releasing hormone and glutamic acid. It is hoped that some of this research will pay off with new and improved medications for panic and related disorders in the very near future.

Appendix A: Commonly Used Medications for Panic Disorder and Agoraphobia

Group	Medications	Action	Problems
Tricyclic antidepressants (TCAs)	Tofranil (imipramine) Elavil (amitriptyline) Sinequan (doxepin) Norpramin (desipramine) Pamelor (nortriptyline)	reduce panic attacks	constipation, blurred vision, dizziness, dry mouth
Serotonin-specific reuptake inhibitors (SSRIs)	Prozac (fluoxetine) Zoloft (sertraline) Paxil (paroxetine) Luvox (fluvoxamine)	reduce panic attacks	can cause sexual dysfunction
Monoamine oxidase inhibitors (MAOIs)	Nardil (phenelzine) Parnate (tranylcypromine)	reduce panic attacks	special diet to avoid tyramine
Benzodiazepine	Xanax (alprazolam)	reduces panic attacks	potentially habituating
Benzodiazepines	Ativan (lorazepam) Tranxene (clorazepate) Klonopin (clonazepam) Valium (diazepam)	reduce general level of anxiety	potentially habituating

Appendix B: Sources for Additional Information

Books

Denise F. Beckfield, Ph.D. *Master Your Panic and Take Back Your Life*. San Luis Obispo, CA: Impact Publishers, 1998.

David Burns, M.D. *Feeling Good*. New York: New American Library, 1980.

The Merck Manual. 15th ed. Rahway, NJ: Merck, Sharp, and Dohme Research Laboratories, 1987.

David Shapiro. *Neurotic Styles*. New York: Basic Books, 1965.

David V. Sheehan, M.D. *The Anxiety Disease*. New York: Bantam Books, 1986.

George Vaillant, M.D. *Adaptation to Life*. Cambridge, MA: Harvard University Press, 1977.

Organizations

National Institute of Mental Health (NIMH)
The Anxiety Disorders Education Program
5600 Fishers Lane
Room 7C-02, MSC 8030
Bethesda, MD 20892
(800) 64-PANIC, (888) 8-ANXIETY, and (301) 443-4513
http://www.nimh.nih.gov/anxiety, http://www.nih.gov.health, and http://www.healthfinder.gov

Further information is available for studies specifically regarding panic disorder and social phobia at (301) 496-6565 and, for those concerned with posttraumatic stress disorder, at (301) 496-4874. For information about ongoing research studies into the genetics of panic disorder, call (301) 496-8977 (ask for Liz Maxwell, LCSW). Further research information is available at the Integrative Neuroscience of Schizophrenia, Mood, and Other Brain Disorders Program at (301) 443-1576 (ask for

Stephen L. Foote, Ph.D.). New investigators interested in research grants can contact the Prevention Research Branch at (301) 443-4283. Potential researchers can also contact Peter Muehrer, Ph.D., at pmuehrer@nih.gov.

American Psychiatric Association
1400 K Street, NW
Washington, DC 20005
(202) 682-6000

Anxiety Disorders Association of America
11900 Parklawn Drive, Suite 100
Rockville, MD 20852-2624
(301) 231-0350

Freedom from Fear
308 Staten Island, NY 10305
(718) 680-1883

Research is currently under way in the area of emotional disorders at the following institutions:

Harvard University
Contact Ronald C. Kessler, Ph.D. (617) 432-3587
or Jill M. Hooley, D.Phil. (617) 495-9508

New York University
Contact Joseph LeDoux, Ph.D. (212) 998-3930

University of Vermont
Contact Bruce Kapp, Ph.D. (802) 656-2670

Emory University
Contact Michael Davis, Ph.D. (404) 727-3591

Boston University
Contact David Barlow, Ph.D. (617) 353-9610

University of Pittsburgh
Contact Mary Katherine Shear, M.D. (412) 624-1340

Yale University
Contact Scott Woods, M.D. (203) 974-7038

Research on several psychiatric and neurobiological disorders and treatments (primarily depression, schizophrenia, Huntington's disease, Alzheimer's disease, AIDS dementia complex, antidepressant treatments, and antipsychotic treatments, with the ongoing development of new studies) is being conducted at

University of Mississippi Medical Center
Division of Neurobiology and Behavior Research
University of Mississippi Medical Center
2500 North State Street
Jackson, MS 39216-4505
(601) 984-5898

Glossary

Acetylcholine A neurotransmitter present in many parts of the body and brain (one of the principal neurotransmitters in the parasympathetic nervous system); blocked by medications described as "anticholinergic." It also serves to transmit nerve impulses to muscles; its activity stops when the enzyme cholinesterase causes its chemical breakdown.

Acidic Contributing hydrogen ions to a chemical solution; the opposite of "basic."

Acute stress disorder A condition similar to posttraumatic stress disorder, but limited to a duration of four weeks and involving symptoms of dissociation.

Adrenaline Epinephrine.

Adrenergic Characterized by the use of epinephrine or similar neurotransmitters, such as norepinephrine.

Agoraphobia A psychiatric disorder commonly occurring with panic disorder. People with this condition fear and try to avoid situations in which finding assistance or extricating themselves would be difficult if symptoms of panic should occur. For many, this involves a fear of leaving home, but sometimes symptoms diminish if they can avoid going out alone.

Agranulocytosis A disorder in which there is a dramatic decrease in the number of certain types of white blood cells (granulocytes), predisposing those who have it to infections, often involving sore throat or dermatological or gastrointestinal problems; sometimes associated with the use of certain psychotropic medications, such as clozapine, carbamazepine, and mirtazapine.

Alkaline Basic; the opposite of acidic; characterized by a neutralizing of the effect of acids.

Allele One of two or more forms of a gene at corresponding locations for given chromosomes; determines genetic transmission.

Amino acid One of the basic carbon-containing chemical building blocks of proteins and peptides; must contain an –NH2 group and a –COOH group.

Amygdala An almond-shaped structure located in the temporal lobe of the brain, near the hippocampus; part of the limbic system.

Anticholinergic Counteracting the activity of acetylcholine.

Anticonvulsant A medication acting to prevent seizures. Many of the mood-stabilizing medications were originally used for this purpose.

Antidepressants Medications used to restore a patient's mood from symptoms of depression.

Antipsychotics Medications that diminish symptoms of psychosis.

Anxiety A condition of nervous unrest, common to some degree in most people, but at times reaching the proportions of a psychiatric disorder; for some it is associated with fear of a future catastrophe, while others may be more vague about such thoughts, having what is referred to as "free-floating anxiety."

Aplastic anemia A serious condition, sometimes related to the use of psychotropic medications (such as carbamazepine), in which the bone marrow shuts down, producing an inadequate supply of red blood cells.

Asymmetry Lacking the same anatomy at equal distances from a point, line, or plane; usually referring to a lack of bilateral symmetry, since many areas are supposed to be anatomically the same at equal distances from a midline plane; often an easy way to spot abnormalities.

Atherosclerotic heart disease The gradual narrowing of the arteries that perfuse the heart muscle. This condition is made worse by several factors, including heredity, high cholesterol levels, hypertension, and emotional stress.

Atrophy A wasting away or gradual decrease in size, as if from lack of nourishment; often indicates disease.

Autonomic nervous system The part of the nervous system

that deals with the regulation of cardiac muscle, smooth muscle, and glands; divided into the sympathetic and parasympathetic nervous systems. It works largely on an unconscious level, and is often affected by emotions.

Autosomal Pertaining to a chromosome other than a sex chromosome.

Basal ganglia Clusters of nerve cells deep in the cerebral hemispheres, consisting on each side of the caudate nucleus, putamen, globus pallidus, amygdala, and claustrum (some people include the thalamus and other nearby structures); tied in with a primitive motor pathway and with the limbic system.

Basic The opposite chemically of "acidic."

Beta blockers Medications that block part of the activity of epinephrine and norepinephrine.

Biomedical model A medical model according to which the patient is dealt with mostly in a biological fashion, with little attention paid to the psychological and social spheres (cf. biopsychosocial model).

Biopsychosocial model A systematic medical model that incorporates factors from biology, psychology, and the patient's social interactions (cf. biomedical model).

Bipolar disorder A mood disorder characterized by episodes of mania at some times and by symptoms of depression at others (formerly called manic-depressive illness).

Brainstem The midbrain, pons, and medulla.

Brief psychotic disorder A psychiatric disturbance lasting less than one month and characterized by delusions, hallucinations, disorganized speech, and/or disorganized behavior (or even catatonia).

Buffer A combination of chemicals that resists changes in pH.

Carbon dioxide A gas that is one of the by-products of metabolism, and which the lungs usually expel. Many researchers believe that if it's in too high a concentration or if the body is overly sensitive to it, this gas can contribute to anxiety and panic.

CAT (or CT) scans See **Imaging studies**.

Catatonia A condition found in several different psychiatric disorders, including schizophrenia, depression, mania, and organic mental disorders; characterized by some combination of stupor, lack of movement, lack of speech, seemingly purposeless overactivity, and stereotyped movements.

Catecholamine One of a group of similar chemical compounds, such as epinephrine, norepinephrine, and dopamine, related to the amino acid L-phenylalanine. Much of the work of the sympathetic nervous system is carried out by means of catecholamines (see **Neurotransmitter** and **Hormone**).

Cell membrane The thin partially permeable layer of material surrounding each of the cells in the body; involved in controlling which chemicals move into and out of the cells.

Cerebellum The part of the brain behind the brainstem concerned with coordination and movement.

Cerebral cortex That portion of the cerebrum located on the outside of the structure and containing nerve cell bodies.

Cerebrospinal fluid (CSF) The fluid formed by the tissue of the brain and the choroid plexus, circulated through the ventricles and in and around the spinal cord and eventually reabsorbed by the veins in and around the brain.

Cerebrum A large part of the brain, consisting of the cerebral cortex, most of the limbic system (except for those parts in the brainstem), corpus callosum (which connects the two hemispheres), pituitary gland, pineal gland, basal ganglia, internal capsule (containing fibers connecting the cerebral cortex with other lower parts of the brain), and thalamus, as well as a few other lesser components. The higher functions of the brain, e.g., thought processes and memory, are located here, especially in the cerebral cortex.

Character The part of the personality that appears to be learned or acquired in the course of life, in contrast to the temperament, which describes the part that is more innate and biological.

Choleric Pertaining to the irritable temperament attributed to yellow bile in humoral theory.

Chromosome One of the structures in the nuclei of living cells containing DNA and responsible for the transmission of genetic information both in cell division and from parents to their offspring.

Cingulate gyrus Part of the cerebrum, usually considered part of the limbic system, surrounding the top of the corpus callosum like a belt.

Cognitive-behavioral therapy Therapy that involves conscious, rational modifications in the way patients think and behave.

Conditioned response Learned reactions, either involuntary responses or voluntary behavior; often involved in the learned component of emotional disorders; amenable to treatment by desensitization.

Corpus callosum Part of the cerebrum, the nerve fibers of which connect the two hemispheres.

Cortex The outer part of an organ, such as the brain or the adrenal gland.

Cytochrome P450 system A class of proteins found in the liver, the gut wall, and other organs, which serves to metabolize away certain chemicals. This system helps dispose of many of the psychotropic medications. Certain other chemicals can impose variations on the system's activity, causing it to work either faster or more slowly.

Defenses Coping mechanisms that help people maintain emotional equilibrium. Some are adaptive, being used by those who manage to deal well with life's ups and downs, but others are dysfunctional, providing a distorted view of reality and only briefly postponing more unhappiness and further problems.

Delirium A temporary organic mental disturbance, characterized by illusions, hallucinations, physical restlessness, and incoherence.

Delusion A false belief caused by a psychiatric disorder.

Dementia An organic mental deterioration involving loss of memory and other higher cortical functions (resulting in, for example, speech disturbance, problems with motor function, difficulty in recognizing people and things, and organizational difficulties); can be a permanent and gradually deteriorating situation or a temporary one (often called "senility" in the elderly).

Denial A primitive, poorly adaptive coping mechanism by which a person tries to disavow the existence of some unpleasant reality.

Depolarization The event occurring when a nerve cell "fires," losing the usual positive charge on the outside of its membrane.

Depression A mood disorder characterized by dejection (often with slowed movements and thinking), loss of enjoyment (anhedonia), excessive feelings of guilt, alterations in sleep and appetite, ruminations about loss and death, and difficulty in concentrating. Treatments include antidepressant medications, psychotherapy, and electroconvulsive therapy.

Desensitization Treatment of emotional reactions by gradual exposure to the troublesome stimulus so that it eventually becomes less bothersome.

Dissociation The separation of certain groups of mental processes from others. It can happen in a variety of psychiatric disorders, such as acute stress disorder, and is frequently seen in panic attacks, manifested as derealization (the feeling that one's surroundings aren't real) or depersonalization (the feeling that one is detached from oneself or that one is not real). Those affected are often unable to remember events surrounding a panic attack or some traumatic event.

Dominant Referring to an allele expressing itself genetically, even if only one such allele is present (on two homologous chromosomes).

Dopamine One of the neurotransmitters in several different parts of the brain, including the limbic system; involved especially in schizophrenia and addictions.

Dopaminergic Having to do with neurotransmission by dopamine.

Dorsal raphé nuclei Clusters of cells that are located in the reticular formation of the midbrain, pons, and medulla, and which produce serotonin, much of it transmitted to the limbic system via the medial forebrain bundle.

Down-regulation A decrease in postsynaptic neurotransmitter receptor activity.

Drug abuse Excessive use of pharmacologically active substances leading to social and/or physical injury to a person.

Drug dependence Excessive use of pharmacologically active substances, usually occurring over a longer period of time than that involved in drug abuse, often involving the development of tolerance, withdrawal symptoms, the need for gradually increasing doses of the substance, a craving for it, the neglecting of other social obligations for it, or the continued use of it in spite of psychological or physical problems that result from overuse.

Echocardiogram An imaging procedure in which sound waves are transmitted into the area of the heart, bounce back, and are reassembled (resembling sonar) to show the shape, size, and movement of the various parts of the heart; often used in checking for mitral valve prolapse.

Electrocardiogram (EKG) A tracing of electrical potentials generated by the heart while it is beating. A technician places electrical leads on several parts of the body to pick up the signals.

Electroconvulsive therapy (ECT) One of the safer and more effective methods of treating depression, despite its bad reputation from earlier times. Currently only done with general anesthesia and muscle relaxant medication, it is often reserved for forms of depression that prove unresponsive to other treatments or that are very severe. In these treatments, which are usually done in a hospital over several days, a controlled electrical current is sent through the patient's brain in such a way as to minimize memory loss and maximize therapeutic effect. Also known as electroshock therapy (EST).

Electroencephalogram (EEG) A written recording of voltage potentials at various points on and about the head, generated by the activity of the nerve cells in the brain; useful for determining certain neurological conditions and for monitoring the progress of ECT.

Empathy The capacity for and act of sensing another person's feelings and thoughts, probably in response to subtle clues given by the other person.

Endocrine Pertaining to glands and tissues that secrete hormones internally.

Enzyme A protein that speeds up a chemical reaction or causes it to occur.

Epinephrine One of the principal hormones in the body, coming from the adrenal medulla. The sympathetic nervous system stimulates its release. It is closely related chemically to norepinephrine, one of the principal neurotransmitters in the brain.

Ergot preparations Chemical derivatives of a fungus that sometimes infects rye and other cereals; used in treating vascular headaches.

Euphoria An abnormal sense of well-being.

Euthymia Emotional tranquillity.

Fight or flight response The emotional and physiological reaction of the body to real or perceived danger; often enlisted as part of a learned, conditioned response to danger more apparent than real.

Fornix A pathway in the limbic system, many of whose fibers lead from the hippocampus to the mamillary bodies; located under the corpus callosum.

Four bodily humors See **Humoral theory**.

G-protein A special protein on the inner surface of the cell membrane that transmits a signal from a neurotransmitter receptor on the outer surface of the membrane, often by generating a chemical called cyclic AMP (the "second messenger").

G-protein-coupled receptors Those neurotransmitter receptor sites associated with the G-proteins.

GABA (gamma-aminobutyric acid) One of the principal neurotransmitters in the brain, inhibitory in nature, and associated with the function of the benzodiazepines.

Glycine One of the less understood neurotransmitters in the brain; tends to be inhibitory in nature.

Gyrus One of the generally rounded convolutions on the surface of the brain.

Habituation Adaptation of an organism to some stimulus; used especially with regard to pharmacological agents when a patient develops tolerance to a medication, requiring more of it for the same effect, and has symptoms of withdrawal when it is removed or reduced in dose. The term is also used in reference to patients getting used to a psychological stimulus, developing a tolerance of it, and then noticing its absence when it is no longer present.

Hallucination The false perception of an external object when no such object is present; hallucinations can be auditory, visual, tactile, olfactory, or gustatory, depending on which sensory modality they are associated with. They are found in several psychiatric disorders, including schizophrenia, profound depression, and mania, and in organic mental disorders such as dementia, delirium, substance intoxication, and substance withdrawal.

Hippocampus Part of the limbic system located close to the amygdala; outgoing nerve fibers from it project through the fornix, notably to the mamillary bodies; its function is tied in closely with the emotions.

Hormone A chemical substance that is produced in the body and that regulates the activity of some organ; similar to neurotransmitters.

Humoral theory An antiquated theory of the emotions

attributing differing temperaments to activity of the four "humors," i.e., yellow bile, black bile, blood, and phlegm.

Hyperpolarization A situation arising after the firing of a nerve cell; after repolarizing, it has a slightly higher positive charge outside the cell membrane than it had in its resting state before firing.

Hypertension A general medical disorder involving persistent elevation of the blood pressure, which predisposes persons having it to heart disease, stroke, kidney disease, and other problems. It can be caused transiently by certain psychotropic medications.

Hyperventilation The tendency to breathe too rapidly and usually too shallowly, so that carbon dioxide is lost through the lungs, making the blood more alkaline; tied in closely with anxiety, and contributing, in turn, to more anxiety.

Hypothalamo-pituitary axis The connection of the brain to secretion by the pituitary gland, governing many bodily functions and tying the emotions into general physiology.

Hypothalamus An area of the brain just under the thalamus, closely tied in with the limbic system and located in proximity to the pituitary gland; deals with activation and integration of the autonomic nervous system, endocrine activity, and many unconscious bodily functions.

Imaging studies The use of various forms of radiation to draw pictures of the brain. These recently developed techniques include computerized axial tomography (CAT or CT scans), magnetic resonance imaging (MRI scans), positron emission tomography (PET scans), and single photon emission computed tomography (SPECT scans). Some of these scans show images that give only details of the anatomy, but others give a picture of brain function as well.

Induction The imposing of an increase in function of some enzyme, such as in the cytochrome P450 system, by chemical means.

Ion A chemical particle carrying an electrical charge.

Ion channel A passageway through the cell membrane, especially of a nerve cell, for selected ions.

Irritable bowel syndrome One of the general medical disorders commonly found in people with panic and other anxiety disorders. The condition is characterized by alternating problems with diarrhea and constipation, frequently involves certain dietary intolerances, and is often exacerbated by stress and troubled emotional states; other symptoms are bloating, nausea, headache, and fatigue.

L-aspartic acid One of the less understood neurotransmitters in the brain; tends to be excitatory in nature.

L-DOPA An amino acid serving as an intermediate product in the conversion of L-phenylalanine into dopamine, norepinephrine, and epinephrine.

L-glutamic acid One of the most prevalent neurotransmitters in the brain; tends to be excitatory in nature (in contrast, for example, to GABA). Research is under way on one of its receptors, the NMDA receptor.

L-phenylalanine One of the amino acids; a precursor to the neurotransmitters dopamine and norepinephrine and the hormones epinephrine and L-thyroxin.

L-thyroxin One of the main hormones produced by the thyroid gland; serves to help regulate the body's overall rate of metabolism.

L-tryptophan An amino acid serving as a precursor to the neurotransmitter serotonin; its abundance in certain foods, such as turkey and tuna, contributes to the drowsy feeling one gets after eating them.

Lactic acid (lactate) One of the metabolic products in the breakdown of sugar, the next step typically involving the release of carbon dioxide. Patients with panic disorder often have induced panic attacks when given lactate intravenously.

Ligand An ion or molecule that forms a special, specific type of chemical bond.

Ligand-gated channels One of the types of ion channels

associated with neurotransmitter receptors and involving the direct attachment of the neurotransmitter to a piece of the protein that is part of the ion channel itself.

Limbic system Structures in the brain, such as the hippocampus, parahippocampal gyrus, amygdala, hypothalamus, cingulate gyrus, fornix, mamillary bodies, and olfactory regions, as well as the septal area, dorsal raphé nuclei, and locus ceruleus, which communicate closely with each other and have a great deal to do with the emotions. (There is some disagreement as to the exact components of this system.)

Lithium The third element in the periodic chart, typically used in the form of lithium carbonate to help stabilize mood swings, especially in bipolar disorder.

Locus ceruleus Groups of cells located in the pons that produce norepinephrine, much of it transmitted to the limbic system via the medial forebrain bundle.

Mamillary bodies Part of the hypothalamus and limbic system, at the forward end of the fornices.

Mania A mood disorder usually characterized by elation, irritability, pressured speech, and increased motor activity. People with this disorder often have grandiose or persecutory delusions, and in their speech jump from one idea to another ("flight of ideas").

Medial forebrain bundle A bidirectional group of fibers connecting areas in the brainstem with other higher areas in the limbic system. Much of the serotonin originating in the brainstem goes through this bundle, ending up in the hippocampus, amygdala, and septal area, as well as in limbic-associated areas.

Medulla The part of the brainstem below the pons and above the beginning of the spinal cord.

Melancholic Pertaining to the sad temperament attributed to "black bile" in humoral theory.

Mesolimbic pathway One of the groups of nerve fibers in the brain carrying dopamine from the substantia nigra, in the midbrain, to the higher limbic areas.

Metabolism The combination of all the chemical and physical processes by which organisms reproduce, grow, and maintain their own existence.

Midbrain Part of the brainstem, beneath the cerebrum and above the pons, containing many ascending and descending nerve fibers, as well as the substantia nigra and the dorsal raphé nuclei.

Migraine headaches Vascular headaches, often involving, in the "classic migraine," a prodrome, which can include strange visual disturbances, before the onset of the headache itself; in "common migraines," there is less tendency for such prodromal symptoms. The word "migraine" is often incorrectly used by nonmedical persons to mean "bad headache."

Mitral valve prolapse A disorder of one of the valves of the heart, in which the leaflets of the mitral valve give way when the heart pumps; can be associated with a number of diseases, including thyroid disturbances, muscular dystrophy, and sickle cell disease, but is also frequently found in people with panic disorder. Symptoms do not always occur, but when they do, they frequently imitate the symptoms of panic disorder.

MK-869 One of the antagonists to substance P currently under research.

Monoamine oxidase An enzyme involved, either directly or indirectly, in the breakdown of several neurotransmitters and hormones, including norepinephrine, epinephrine, dopamine, and serotonin.

Monoamine oxidase inhibitors (MAOIs) Medications that inhibit the activity of monoamine oxidase and that are used in the treatment of panic disorder and depression. Examples include phenelzine (Nardil), tranylcypromine (Parnate), and isocarboxazid (Marplan).

MRI scans See **Imaging studies**.

Neocortex The "new cortex" part of the brain, less characteristic architecturally of the cortices of more primitive life forms.

Neuroleptic The older type of "typical" antipsychotic medications.

Neuroleptic malignant syndrome A disorder caused by antipsychotic medications (usually the older ones), in which the patient's muscles become very stiff, and there is a clouding of consciousness with a high fever. If this potentially fatal condition occurs, the doctor has to take the patient off the offending medicine and sometimes give medications to reverse the antipsychotic's antagonism to dopamine (confusion may result because of the disorder's resemblance to catatonia, for which antipsychotics are one of the treatments).

Neuron An individual nerve cell.

Neurosis An old-fashioned and vague, although useful, term for an emotional disorder charactereized by unresolved psychodynamic conflicts, but not involving reality distortion as severe as that found in psychosis (i.e., any distortion of reality is more one of quantity than of quality).

Neurotransmitter A chemical that serves to transmit impulses from one nerve cell to another (currently including serotonin, norepinephrine, dopamine, GABA, glycine, L-glutamic acid, L-aspartic acid, and substance P).

Noradrenergic Pertaining to neurotransmission by means of norepinephrine.

Norepinephrine One of the principal neurotransmitters in the body; related closely to the sympathetic nervous system. Much of it in the brain comes from the locus ceruleus.

Nucleus A cluster of nerve cells in the brain.

Nucleus accumbens Part of the basal ganglia (specifically the cluster of nerve cells between the head of the caudate nucleus and the putamen); one of the structures in the brain receiving dopaminergic transmission from the substantia nigra by way of the mesolimbic pathway.

Organic Stemming from physical or chemical derangement, either permanent or temporary, of the brain itself.

Paleocortex The "old cortex" part of the brain, involving much of the limbic system and characteristic architecturally of the cortices of more primitive life forms.

Panic A sudden overpowering fright.

Panic attack An episode of intense anxiety, often involving symptoms usually associated with heart problems, such as a racing pulse, heart palpitations, or actual chest pain, as well as sensations of shortness of breath and choking. Victims frequently complain of profuse sweating, trembling or shaking all over, nausea and dizziness, numbness and tingling sensations, and hot and cold flashes, as well as feelings of derealization (the sense that their environment is not real) and depersonalization (the sense that they themselves are not real). Affected persons often feel as though they are losing control or "going crazy." These symptoms can occur in a variety of psychiatric disorders and general medical conditions, but serve as one of the hallmarks of panic disorder. Panic attacks often come on "out of the blue," but sometimes anxiety-provoking factors contribute to their onset.

Panic disorder A psychiatric disorder involving distinct episodes of intense anxiety (panic attacks), which develop abruptly and seemingly without any adequate precipitating event. These episodes, which tend to reach highest intensity over a period of a few minutes and last for an unpredictable amount of time, cause consternation to those affected partly because of their unpredictability. Some people, however, also have panic attacks and anxiety triggered by certain situations, and these individuals restrict their activities in an effort to avoid such provocations (agoraphobia).

Parasympathetic Pertaining to that part of the autonomic nervous system which functions, generally, in opposition to the activity of the sympathetic nervous system, in that it promotes such activities as digestion and tends to slow the heart; it is the opposite of the "fight or flight" response and is associated generally with the release of acetylcholine at target destinations.

Personality The behavioral, cognitive, and emotional patterns characteristic of an individual, to some degree acquired and to some degree the product of innate tendencies.

PET scans See **Imaging studies**.

pH (power of hydrogen) A logarithmic scale for expressing how acidic or basic substances are.

Phlegmatic Pertaining to the apathetic temperament attributed to phlegm in humoral theory.

Pituitary gland A gland at the base of the brain connected to the hypothalamus, partially composed of epithelial tissue; produces numerous hormones affecting the thyroid gland, the adrenal glands, and the kidneys, as well as the overall growth of the body; is tied in closely with limbic function through the hypothalamus.

Platelet (thrombocyte) A tiny blood cell involved in the formation of a blood clot (thrombus). Too much of a decrease in their number can predispose a person to bleeding disorders.

Polarization The natural resting state of a nerve cell, with a slightly more positive electrical voltage outside the cell membrane than inside.

Pons The part of the brainstem between the midbrain and the medulla.

Postsynaptic After the synapse.

Presynaptic Before the synapse.

Prodrome The preliminary symptoms experienced by a patient before a classic migraine or a seizure.

Psychiatry A medical specialty involving the diagnosis and treatment of disorders of emotions, thoughts, cognition, and behaviors.

Psychoanalysis A form of psychotherapy (and the theory it rests on) originating in the work and observations of

Sigmund Freud, a Viennese psychiatrist, who believed in unconscious (and preconscious) mental processes that compete with each other and determine coping mechanisms (defenses), such as repression; involves resolution of transference with the therapist.

Psychodynamic Related to the forces hypothesized to operate in the mind, such as instincts in opposition to inhibitions, or desires in opposition to a sense of reality; describes a certain type of psychotherapy.

Psychosis A psychiatric disorder characterized by a breakdown in a patient's grasp on reality, often involving hallucinations, delusions, disrupted train of thought, and/or disorganized or bizarre behavior (such as catatonia).

Psychotherapy A form of treatment for psychiatric disorder in which a professional alliance is established between a patient and a trained therapist, constructively to modify maladaptive thoughts, feelings, and behaviors. There are many different forms, some relying on the patient's insight into his or her condition and others much more directive in nature.

Psychotropic Pertaining primarily to medications for the treatment of psychiatric disorders.

Rebound The tendency in many physiological mechanisms to overcompensate in the opposite direction when some stimulus disappears; often seen when medications are discontinued (e.g., patients who stop using sedating medications frequently feel overly excitable for a brief period).

Receptors Structures found on the surfaces of cells that neurotransmitters and hormones trigger to effect changes in cell physiology; e.g., neurotransmitters combine with receptors on the surface of nerve cells in transmitting nerve impulses.

Recessive Referring to an allele deficient at expressing itself genetically, unless two such alleles are present (one each, on homologous chromosomes).

Repression An unconscious coping mechanism in which the

mind pushes from awareness ideas and impulses that it finds unacceptable (considered less adaptive than "suppression," in which troubling ideas, impulses, and emotions are consciously pushed to the back of the mind).

Reserpine An early medicine used for the treatment of hypertension and also as a tranquilizer. It tended to deplete the body's store of catecholamines, contributing to symptoms of depression.

Sanguine Pertaining to the optimistic temperament attributed to blood in humoral theory.

Schizophrenia A psychiatric disorder lasting for at least six months, involving some combination of hallucinations, delusions, speech disorganization, disorganized behavior (such as catatonia), or a general lack of speech, facial expression, or volition, and associated with a deterioration of ability in a person's public or private life.

Second messenger system A system of intermediate intracellular chemical messengers serving to communicate between a neurotransmitter (or hormone) and the ultimate ion channel target; usually involves the chemicals cyclic adenosine monophosphate (cAMP), cyclic guanosine monophosphate (cGMP), calcium, or metabolites of phosphatidylinositol.

Septal area A group of nerve cells located at the base of the septum pellucidum; the part of the limbic system associated with the perception of pleasure.

Serotonergic Pertaining to neurotransmission by means of serotonin.

Serotonin A vasoconstrictor neurotransmitter found in the brain, as well as in several other body tissues. It is enzymatically formed from the amino acid L-tryptophan, and is one of the major neurotransmitters in the brain, principally transmitted from the dorsal raphé nuclei into the limbic system, where it helps to modulate mood.

Serotonin-specific reuptake inhibitors (SSRIs) Certain of the newer antidepressants and antipanic medications that block the reuptake of serotonin specifically into the presynaptic nerve cell (e.g., fluoxetine, sertraline, paroxetine, fluvoxamine, and citalopram).

Social phobia A psychiatric disorder in which persons have a pervasive fear that they will humiliate themselves in a social or performance situation; because of the resulting anxiety, they characteristically come to avoid such situations, restricting their lives accordingly.

SPECT scans See **Imaging studies.**

Spike threshold The voltage at which a nerve cell fires. The voltage across the cell membrane reaches this point once electrical and chemical events cause the nerve cell's polarization to be reduced a certain amount.

Stress Stimuli interfering with an organism's function by disturbing its emotional or physiological equilibrium; a major contributing factor in the development of psychiatric disorders, as well as of general medical disorders such as heart disease, high blood pressure, asthma, rheumatoid arthritis, irritable bowel syndrome, and peptic ulcer disease. Stress also damages the body's immune response, and is thought to be linked, to some degree, to the development of cancer.

Substance P A peptide found in the brain seemingly related to the development of depression and to a person's level of stress. It seems to function in an unconventional manner, without direct involvement in serotonin, norepinephrine, or dopamine circuits.

Substance P antagonist (SPA) A medication that opposes the depressant action of substance P.

Substantia nigra A layer of grayish substance in the midbrain which produces dopamine destined for several areas of the brain, including the limbic system and the basal ganglia.

Substrate The chemical upon which an enzyme works.

Sympathetic Pertaining to that part of the autonomic nervous system that functions primarily adrenergically at its target destination; associated with delivery of epinephrine and norepinephrine. Tending to work in opposition to the parasympathetic nervous system, it is tied in closely with the "fight or flight" response and is overly active in panic attacks.

Synapse A region of proximity and functional connection by means of neurotransmitters between two nerve cells.

Target symptoms Symptoms which a medication is specifically designed to alleviate.

Temperament The contribution to the personality that appears to be hereditary.

Thalamus Part of the brain located deep to the cortex, considered by some to be part of the basal ganglia, and functioning as the principal relay center for sensory signals from the body and for impulses from other parts of the brain.

Thrombocytopenia A decrease in the number of platelets (thrombocytes), resulting in an increase in bleeding tendencies; found in several illnesses and can occur with the use of certain psychotropic medications, such as valproic acid.

Transference The unconscious tendency for a patient in psychoanalysis to feel about, think about, and act toward a therapist as though the therapist were someone from the patient's past or from other parts of his or her life.

Tricyclic antidepressants (TCAs) An older type of antidepressant medication, effective but typically with a number of troublesome side effects; still quite useful in selected cases of panic disorder.

Type A personality A designation referring to people who place much emphasis on meeting deadlines and "beating the clock" and who tend to be perfectionists and to feel a great deal of frustration in daily life. They appear to be prone to premature atherosclerotic heart disease and to other medical and psychiatric disturbances.

Type B personality A designation referring to people who are more relaxed than those with type A personality; such people have less need to be perfectionistic and are not so bothered by deadlines and daily frustrations.

Up-regulation An increase in postsynaptic neurotransmitter receptor activity.

Ventricle One of the cavities in the brain, filled with cerebrospinal fluid and communicating with one another as well as with the central canal of the spinal cord.

Index